D1823806

Felt Gifts and Toys

Felt Gifts and Toys

Anna Griffiths

B T BATSFORD LIMITED

Filmset by Servis Filmsetting Limited, Manchester
Printed in Great Britain by
William Clowes and Sons Limited, Beccles, Suffolk
for the Publishers
B T Batsford Limited
4 Fitzhardinge Street
London W1H 0AH

Contents

Introduction

Everyone has a little experience of felt, using it in kit form to make a stuffed animal, sewing needle cases for presents or even just handling its soft warmth in shops. The bright glowing colours make it a very attractive material for presents and bazaar items which sell quickly. This book has ideas in it to make useful as well as decorative gifts. The very simple things can easily be made by children who have a limited sewing ability.

Most felt sold in shops is about 184 cm (72 in.) wide or cut to 92 cm (36 in.). These widths are sold by the yard and you can also buy squares roughly corresponding to these sizes: 60 cm (24 in.), 45 cm (18 in.), 30 cm (12 in.), and 22 cm (9 in.).

Felt manufacturers have a vast range of colours; it is a good idea to get several of your favourite colours and one or two basics like flesh pink of which one never seems to have enough, for hands and faces. My own felt box has hundreds of pieces, all different sizes and colours. I cannot resist buying a few more squares every time I go into a shop.

Felt is not a woven fabric: it is made from woollen fibres arranged layer upon layer and beaten whilst wet with warm soapy water to interlock the fibres. Dry cleaning or dry cleaning fluids are the only really successful ways of cleaning felt, for washing only matts the fibres more and the material pulls out of shape.

Most of the patterns in this book are simple. For some of the things that you make, you may need to use your patterns again and again and tracing paper is not very strong. Thin card is easier to trace round and you can keep the patterns for extensive future use.

Mark on each pattern piece the number of pieces to be cut out and any sewing directions. Fasten the pattern pieces together with a paper clip or keep them in an envelope for safety.

You do not need to leave a seam allowance on the pattern pieces as felt does not fray, neither is there a 'right' or 'wrong' side. To mark round the pattern pieces on the felt, use a soft pencil or tailor's chalk. When you cut the pieces out, cut on the inside of the pencil or chalk mark. Try to keep the stitches even but not tight when sewing the seams, or else the edges will pucker.

The toys in the book graduate from a simple ball to free standing dolls. They will look neater if you leave an opening for stuffing in the least noticeable place. Try not to overstuff as they become very hard and look strained at the seams.

Felt is easy to handle, it does not slip and slide about so, unless you are very cautious, sewing can be tackled directly after pinning.

Most of the items in this book can be embellished with embroidery, beads, sequins, and metallic threads. Keep the decoration simple to start with and limit the colour scheme to two applied colours; when you get braver you can go on to more riotous colour.

Equipment

The essential items needed for making felt things in this book are listed below:

Felt, available from most stores and handicraft shops

A sharp pair of scissors

Pinking shears for decorative edges

Tracing paper or typing copy paper for tracing off patterns

Needles, sewing and embroidery

Sewing thread and embroidery silk

Stuffing — this can be kapok, cottonwool, synthetic fibre or even old washed and shredded nylon tights or stockings

There are several glues available that stick felt very well. Recommended brands are: *Copydex, UHU, Bostik, Evostik, Resin W., Dufix* and *Marvin Medium.*

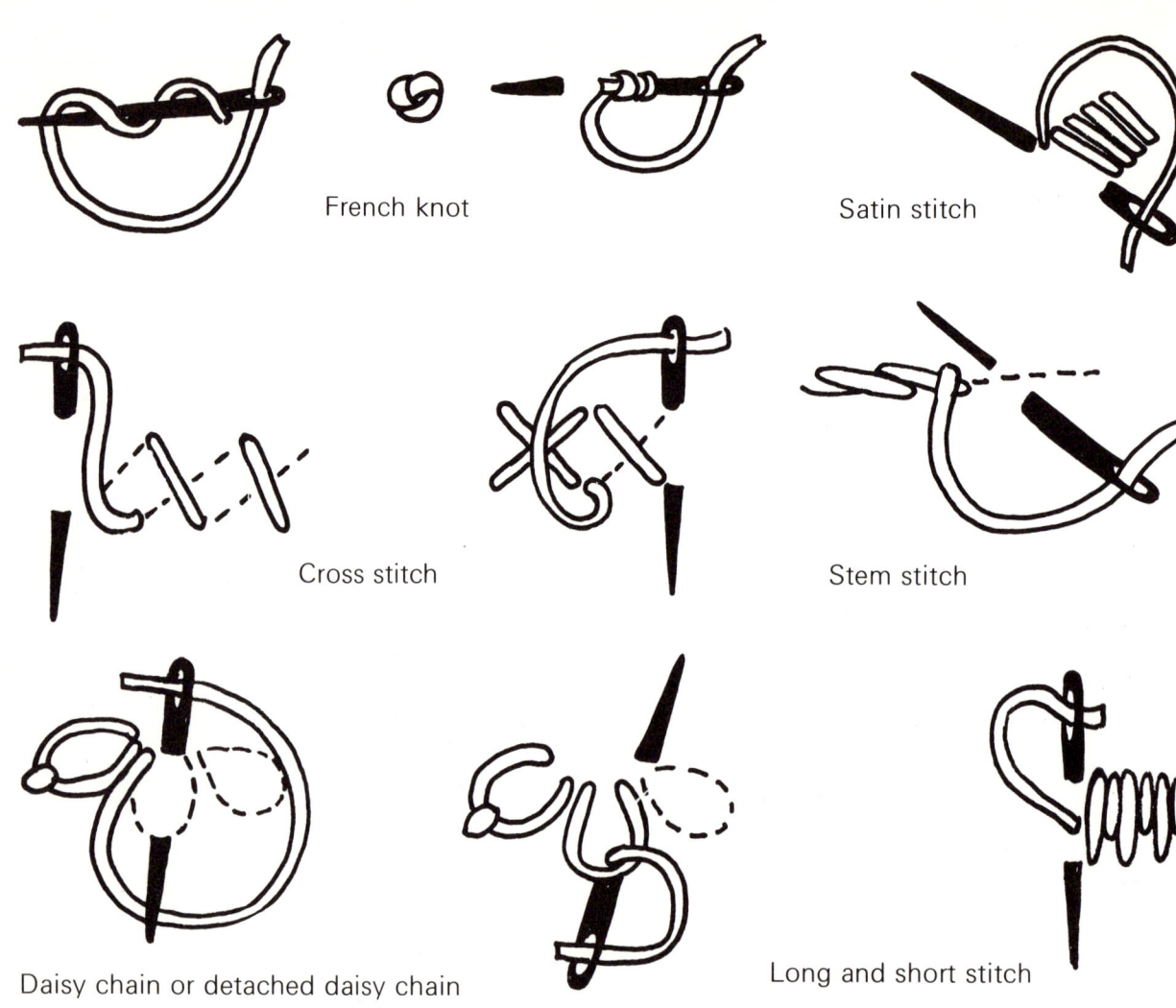

French knot

Satin stitch

Cross stitch

Stem stitch

Daisy chain or detached daisy chain

Long and short stitch

Herringbone stitch

Decorative stitches for felt work

Bookmarkers

Bookmarkers are simply made from one piece of felt 180 mm (7 in.) by 38 mm (1½ in.) and small scraps in contrasting colours.

Use the drawings on the opposite page as patterns, and trace the outline onto a thin piece of paper through which the drawing can be seen, and cut out the shapes.

To make the flower bookmarker, cut the main piece of felt 180 mm (7 in.) by 38 mm (1½ in.) using the pattern pieces traced and cut out; lay the flower shape onto a small piece of felt, draw round it with a soft pencil and cut out. Using a different coloured felt, lay the leaf shapes on it, draw round and cut out. Position the flower and leaves on the bookmarker, glue the backs of the pieces, and stick them down. To complete the bookmarker, cut a fringe 25 mm (about 1 in.) up from the bottom.

Other ideas for simple motifs could be a tree, a star, a heart or a ship.

These bookmarker ideas are actual size and can be
used as trace patterns

Egg Cosies

Egg cosies are still used in a great many homes and they make very attractive place settings for an Easter morning breakfast table. Here are three egg cosies: a simple basic one with a star motif, a two-piece cosy with a floral pattern, and a cockerel.

To make the three-piece egg cosy, use the pattern on page 14, and cut three shapes either in the same coloured felt or different colours. Using matching thread or stranded embroidery silk, sew the sides together with blanket stitch. Cut three stars from contrasting felt and stitch or stick one on each side of the cosy.

For the floral two-piece cosy, use the trace pattern on page 14. Cut two sides in matching or contrasting felt. Sew up the sides as in the previous cosy, and then cut the bottom either with pinking shears or making scallops along the edge with ordinary scissors. Cut the flower shapes and leaves using the pattern shown and stick or stitch in place.

To make the cockerel cosy. Trace the pattern pieces from page 15. Use red felt for the comb and wattle, and white felt for the head. Two black beads are needed for the eyes.

Cut one comb and two wattles in red felt. Cut two head shapes in white felt. Place the comb in between the two head shapes in the position marked, pin into place and sew with small running stitches all the way round the head, making sure that the comb is securely attached. Take the wattle pieces and sew them together at the junction marked with an arrow on the pattern. Place the wattle in position under the beak and pin the piece for the eyes either side of the head. Sew in place with running stitches where shown. Sew a bead on either side with matching thread. Cut the bottom edge of the cosy with pinking shears, or make a pointed edge pattern with ordinary scissors.

Egg cosies
Right   Using the outline as a pattern, cut 3 basic
shapes and 3 stars in contrasting felt
Below   Cut 2 basic shapes and one floral motif using
the outline as trace patterns

Cockerel cosy and pattern

Comb
cut 1 (in red)

Head
cut 2 (in white)

Wattle
cut 2 (in red)

Position on the
dotted line marked
on the head
Sew eyes the X mark

Pincushions

Felt pincushions always sell fast at bazaars and fetes. They are easy to make and provide an opportunity to create something imaginative at little cost. Here are instructions for five pincushions.

Almost anything can be used for stuffing pincushions: kapok, cotton-wool, sawdust, etc, but to be really professional, save the bean grounds from your next pot of coffee. Dry them and pour them into the cushion — it may be better to leave a smaller hole then usual. This may seem more tedious then just pushing any old stuffing in, but the advantage of coffee bean grounds is that they keep the pins from getting rusty as they do not hold moisture.

The flower drum is the simplest pincushion to make first.

Cut a piece of felt 220 mm (8½ in.) by 50 mm (2 in.). Join the short sides together by oversewing with matching thread.

Cut circles 64 mm (2½ in.) in diameter. Pin one in the top of the felt ring just made and one in the bottom. Oversew each one in, leaving a small opening to put the stuffing in. Stuff and sew up.

Cut the flowers of different shapes and sizes to cover the sides of the drum. These can be sewn or stuck on.

The heart pincushion is to be worn on the wrist. It is a useful aid when machine sewing or putting up hems and saves carrying pins from one place to another — they are there on a neat wristband.

This requires a small piece of felt about 150 mm (6 in.) by 100 mm (4 in.). Cut a paper heart from a piece of paper and use this as the pattern. If

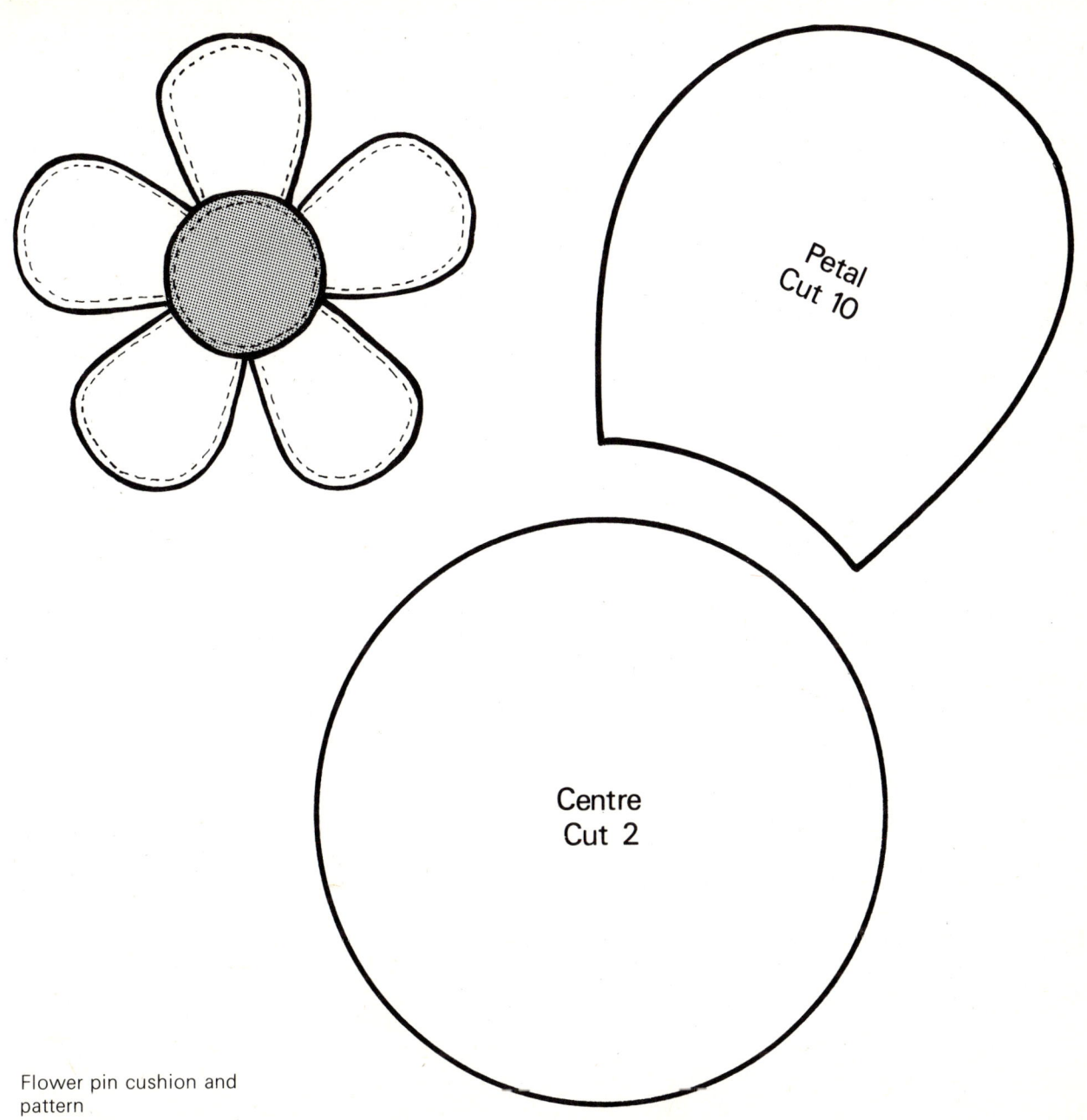

Petal
Cut 10

Centre
Cut 2

Flower pin cushion and
pattern

it is made about 64 mm (2½ in.) at the widest point it will fit into the felt square three times.

Using the pattern, draw three hearts on the felt and cut them out. Elastic, wide tape or ribbon can be used for the wristband. Take the wrist measurement and add a small amount for overlapping. Sew on a press fastener to close the band and neaten the edges if necessary.

Position two of the hearts centrally on the band and sew firmly in place.

Put the remaining heart on top of the others and sew round the edge with a neat firm oversewing stitch leaving a gap for the stuffing.

Put in the stuffing and sew up the gap.

Decorate the top heart with french knots or cross-stitch patterns.

To make the flower pincushion a 350 mm (12 in.) square of orange felt and a 230 mm (9 in.) square of green felt are needed.

Trace the pattern pieces from page 17.

Using the petal pattern, draw round it on the orange felt ten times then cut them out either with pinking shears or ordinary scissors.

Cut out two green felt centres using the pattern.

Place the petals together in pairs and sew them together with a running stitch a short distance in from the edge. The petals are not stuffed; if this is desired, it would be better to use a tighter stitch for the sewing together, as running stitch is too widely spaced.

Take one of the green circles and place the petals around the outer edge. When they are equally spaced, pin them and sew in place.

Place the other circle on the top and pin.

Sew all round through all thicknesses with a neat backstitch, leaving a small space for the stuffing. Push the stuffing in very firmly and sew up the gap.

The top of the cushion could be decorated with cross-stitch patterns or satin stitch flowers in bright colours.

You will need 76 mm × 102 mm (3 in. × 4 in.) or 25 mm × 229 mm (1 in. × 9 in.) square scraps of felt in two or more colours, and 127 mm (5 in.) of narrow ribbon.

Cut 3 brim circles in felt. From one circle cut out a central hole 19 mm ($\frac{3}{4}$ in.) in diameter and keep the circle. Cut out one crown shape. Place the edges of the crown together to form a tube, sew this seam up. Sew the small felt circle into the narrowest end of the crown. Place the crown over the circle with the hole and sew in place firmly. Position the remaining brim circles under the completed hat. Blanket stitch the three circles together for 64 mm ($2\frac{1}{2}$ in.) and continue the blanket stitch all round the rim of the top circle.

Put the narrow ribbon round the base of the crown and stick in place. Cut out 5 flowers and 5 centres and three leaves. Stick these around the brim and base of the crown.

Push in a thimble inside the crown, and your needles in the bottom layers of the hat.

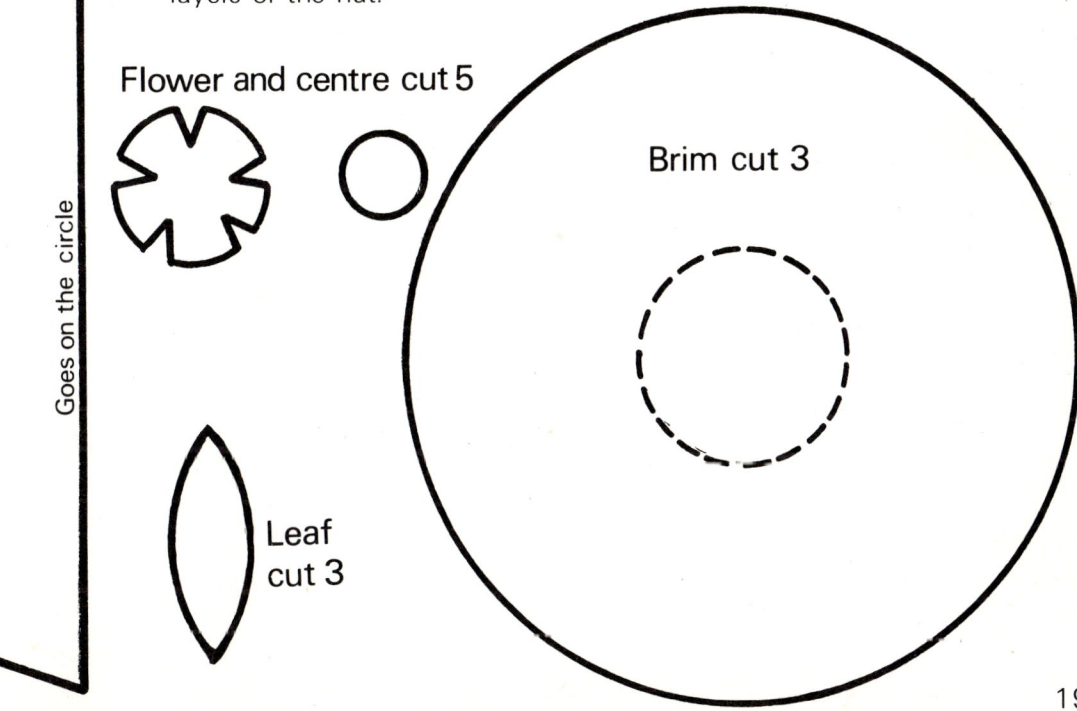

Crown cut 1

Goes on the circle

Flower and centre cut 5

Brim cut 3

Leaf cut 3

To make the fish pincushion a small piece of yellow felt and scraps of orange felt are required. Three fish can be made from one 230 mm (9 in.) square of yellow felt.

Trace the pattern opposite.

Cut two yellow fish shapes.

Cut about ten scales — more can be used if preferred — the fins, and two eyes in orange felt.

Place a fin at the top and one at the bottom of one of the fish. Pin in place and sew.

Place the other fish on top and sew through all thicknesses with a neat backstitch leaving the tail end open.

Push the stuffing in through the tail end, and sew up 19 mm ($\frac{3}{4}$ in.) from the edge.

Cut the tail in a fringe as shown.

Stick on the scales and the eyes.

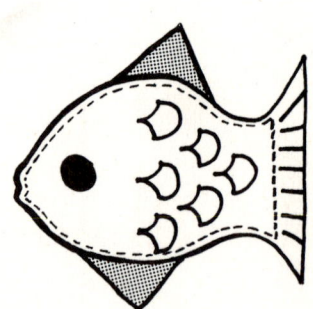

To make the hedgehog, materials needed are a small piece of lilac felt (a 230 mm (9 in.) square will make three) and a scrap of navy felt for the ears.

Trace the pattern opposite.

Cut two sides and one base from the lilac felt and two ears from the navy felt.

Oversew the sides together leaving the straight base edge open. Pin in the base and oversew all round leaving a small opening.

Put in the stuffing and sew up.

Position the ears and sew them in place at the base.

Embroider the nose with black thread and make a french knot on each side for the eyes.

Push pins in to complete the hedgehog's spines.

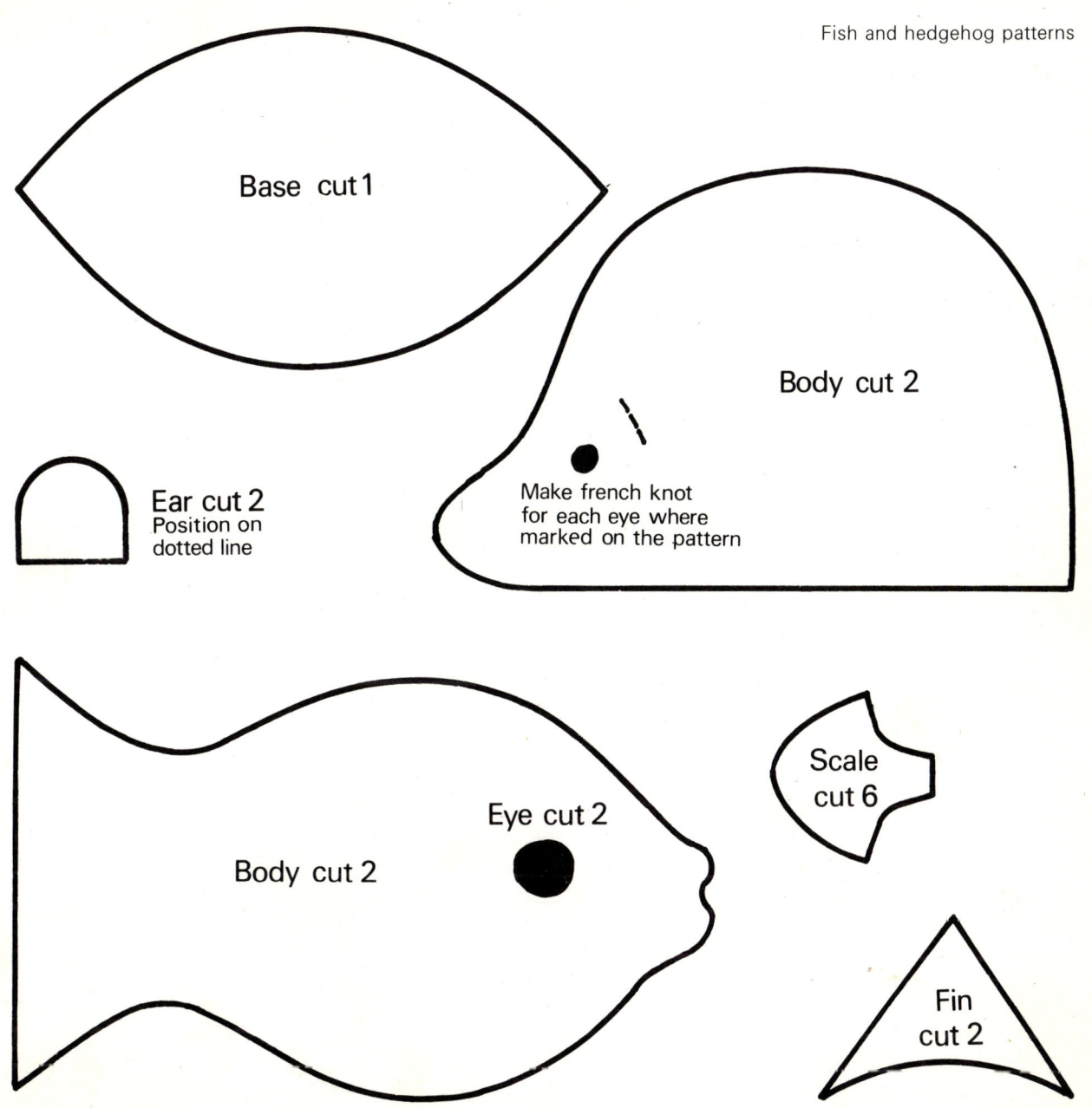

Base cut 1

Body cut 2

Ear cut 2
Position on
dotted line

Make french knot
for each eye where
marked on the pattern

Eye cut 2

Scale
cut 6

Body cut 2

Fin
cut 2

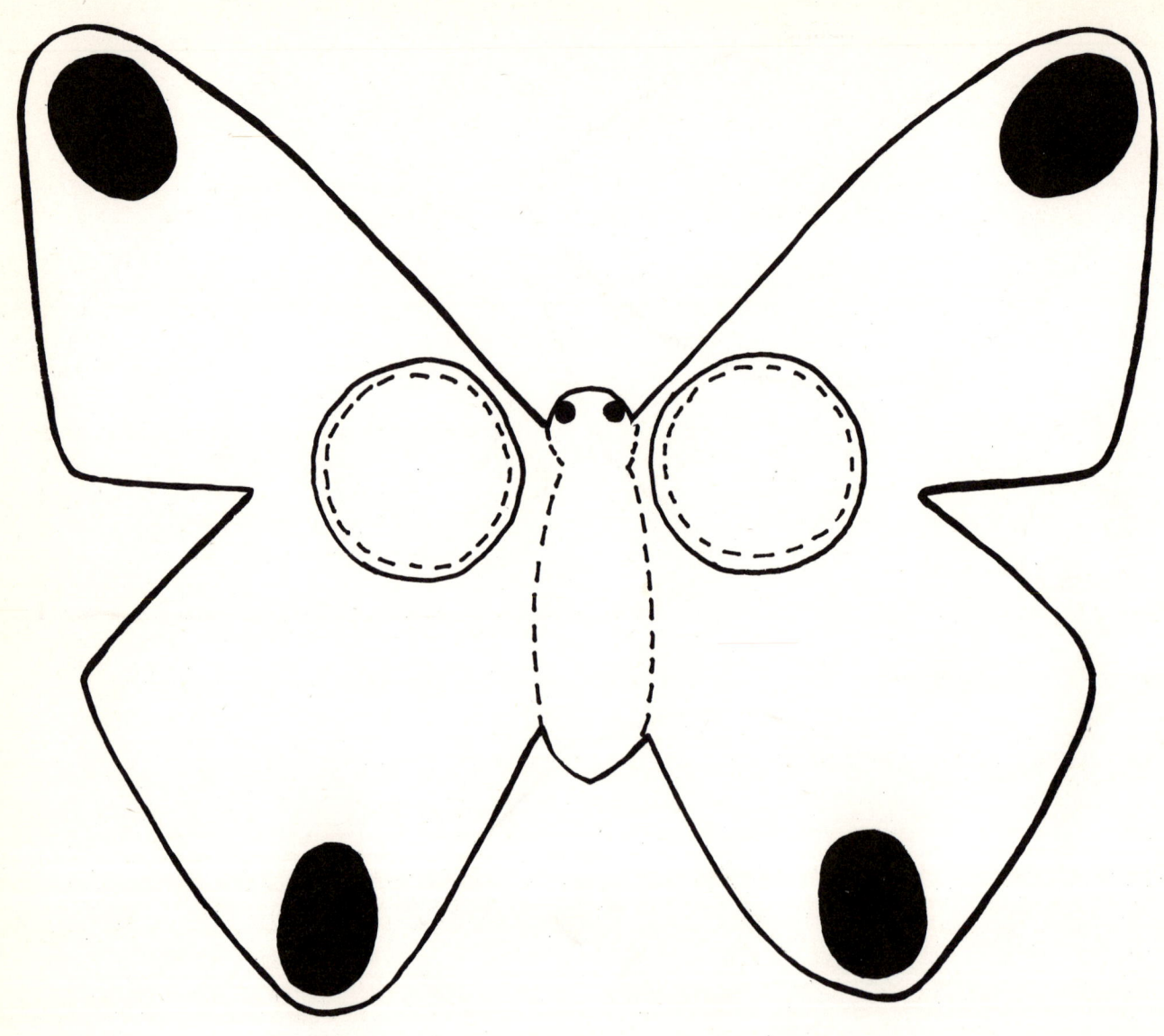

Pattern for butterfly needlecase. Cut 2 main shapes,
each one place on a fold

(Butterfly needlecase)

The Butterfly needlecase on page 22 serves two purposes. Apart from being decorative, the body is stuffed so that it can hold pins. The wings are used as a needlecase.

Use the trace pattern below to make your paper pattern of the wings and the spots.

You need two different coloured squares of felt and some small pieces in other colours for the spots.

Cut out two butterfly shapes, one in each colour.

Place the two shapes together and oversew all round through both thicknesses, except for the tail end of the body, this is where you stuff the body. The shape of the body is made by backstitching the outline neatly through both layers of felt. To stuff the body, push in some stuffing from the tail end and make it fairly solid, then sew up the end.

Cut out 4 spots for the wings and two circles, using the trace pattern. Sew the circles into place with a simple running stitch, place the spots on the wings and sew these down with long oversewing stitches.

Make two eyes on the head with french or bullion knots.

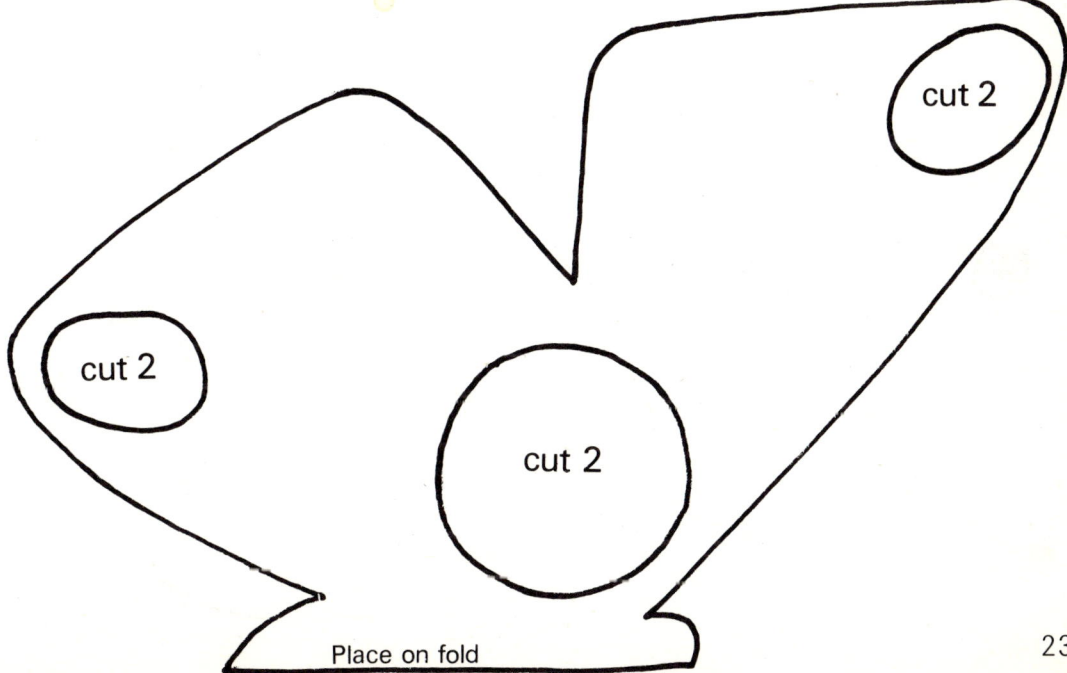

cut 2

cut 2

cut 2

Place on fold

Spectacle Cases

Spectacle cases make useful gifts and are easy to make. The basic pattern is given on page 26. Using this as the starting-point for a variety of different designs, special cases could be made for friends and relatives.

Try to bear in mind the person who will be using the spectacle case when choosing a colour for it; the design might also be influenced by this. There are some ideas for different designs opposite. Trace the basic pattern onto paper and draw round it several times onto drawing paper or even newspaper, so that several designs can be worked out before the felt is bought. If the felt is thin, it can be used double with a different colour inside, and the edges can be pinked or oversewn together.

For a simple spectacle case make a paper pattern, cut it out and place on the felt chosen. Draw round the pattern twice. Cut the two shapes out and place the halves together.

The side seams are sewn up to the points shown on the pattern with a small running stitch or with neat oversewing.

The motif that is applied on top can be the moon and stars shown in the pattern on page 26, or one of your own invention. The cut motifs can be caught down with matching thread or stuck in place.

If you want to be more ambitious with the design, embroidery with contrasting thread or beads can be sewn on to add richness.

Ideas for appliquéd spectacle cases

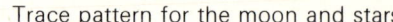

Trace pattern for the moon and stars

The top edge is open from here to here

Simple Purses

Purses in bright pretty designs can be made very quickly from a rectangle of felt. Pin up the sides, leaving just under one third for the flap-over. The fastening can be edge-to-edge like *Velcro* strip, big press-stud fasteners, or even buttons. The decoration on the purses can be a simple ribbon appliqué (see page 28) which is caught down invisibly with small hem stitches at the edges. Tapestry wool embroidery in a simple pattern can be very effective, while an extra band of colour appliquéd onto the edges can strengthen the over-all design.

Floral shapes glued on to the flap of a purse, and a simple embroidery stitch along the edge can make a plain purse look special (see page 29). Sequins sewn on individually or in strips turns a simple flap-over purse into a fashionable evening accessory or a pretty present for a child's party.

Ribbon appliqué

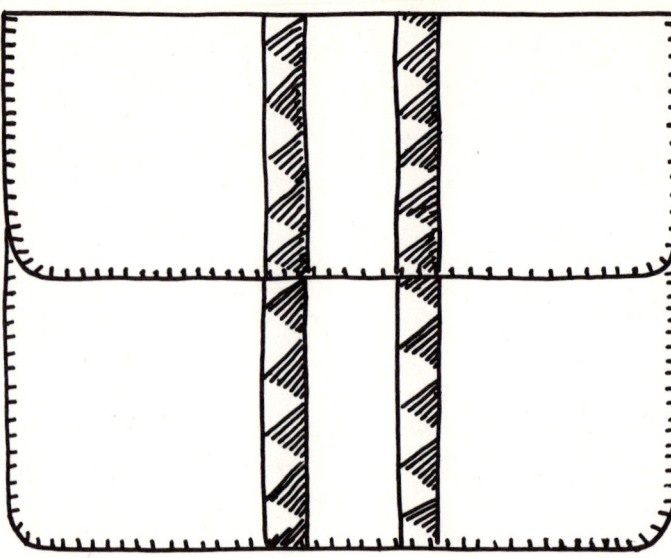

Wool embroidery

Stuck felt appliqué

Sequins sewn on

Make a shoulder bag as shown on page 31 from two squares 30 cm $\times$ 30 cm (12 in. $\times$ 12 in.) and 1·829 m (2 yds) of cotton cord 12 mm ($\frac{1}{2}$ in.) thick. Sew up three sides of the two squares, placed exactly together. Cut 30 cm (12 in.) off the cord. Wind a piece of cotton several times round each cut end of it, and finish with a few stitches to hold in place. This prevents the cord from fraying. Now fasten the cord to the bottom of the bag with oversewing stitch. Take the remaining length of cord, and make a knot 125 mm (5 in.) from the end. Straighten out the loose strands to form the tassels. Oversew the cord to the bag sides, starting from the tassel ends and working up to the top of the bag. Finally, stitch each knot to the ends of the cord that runs along the bottom of the bag. Thick wool cross-stitch patterns or stuck appliquéd designs could be a decorative finish to this design.

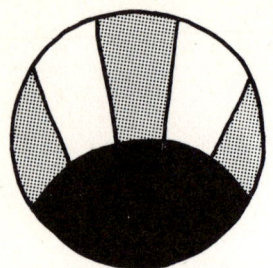

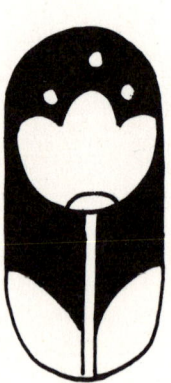

Felt Jewellery

Using felt to make bright cheerful jewellery will not cost very much and could provide a good deal of fun; there are some ideas opposite.

Jewellery findings are on sale quite cheaply in craft shops and big stores. Buy some to make a brooch or a pair of earrings. Choose a slightly thicker felt for the surround and cut the decorative pattern from thinner felt. Stick the pattern pieces on with strong adhesive and then stick the earring or brooch onto the finding, allow it to dry quite thoroughly. Then it is ready to wear.

Make a choker from a strip of felt, which should be the neck measurement plus an inch or two to overlap. Cut out the decorative pattern and stick it on, then sew a press fastener on to close the choker at the back.

Headbands can be made in the same way as the choker, but should be slightly smaller in length, with a piece of elastic sewn in to complete the circle. The possibilities are only as limited as your imagination. Jewellery to match several different outfits will not break the bank, as the quantity of felt used is very small.

Extra vitality can be added to these two dimensional articles by sticking or sewing on matching sequins or very shiny beads, with details perhaps picked out in tiny jet or crystal beads.

Other ideas for fun felt jewellery are to make stuffed fruits and vegetables, and to use them separately, sewn onto jumpers, coat lapels, hats, shoes or with several put together as a necklace or on a bag or basket.

Felt fruits are simple to make. Trace the shapes from the graph and follow the instructions on pages 34 to 41.

Strawberry

Red and green felt. A few small orange beads for the seeds. Stuffing.

Cut 1 strawberry in red.

Cut 1 leaf in green.

Cut 1 stalk in green.

Sew up the side, the bottom and the top two darts, stuff and sew up the opening. Sew on the centre at the top, then roll up the stem and sew along the edge to form a tight roll. Sew the end onto the leaf to complete the strawberry shape. Sew the beads at intervals all over the strawberry to look like seeds.

The strawberry choker on page 34 looks very effective worn over a sweater or in the neckline of a simple dress. You make it by sewing three strawberries to a band of felt as shown on page 36. This must be your neck dimension and about 38 mm ($1\frac{1}{2}$ in.) wide, roll it lengthwise into a tight sausage and sew it firmly in place with small oversewing stitches. Work a loop in buttonhole stitch at one end and sew on a button of the appropriate size the other end. Add a green leaf and sew the veins on with embroidery thread. Sew on the three strawberries, centrally placed, to make an interesting neck ornament.

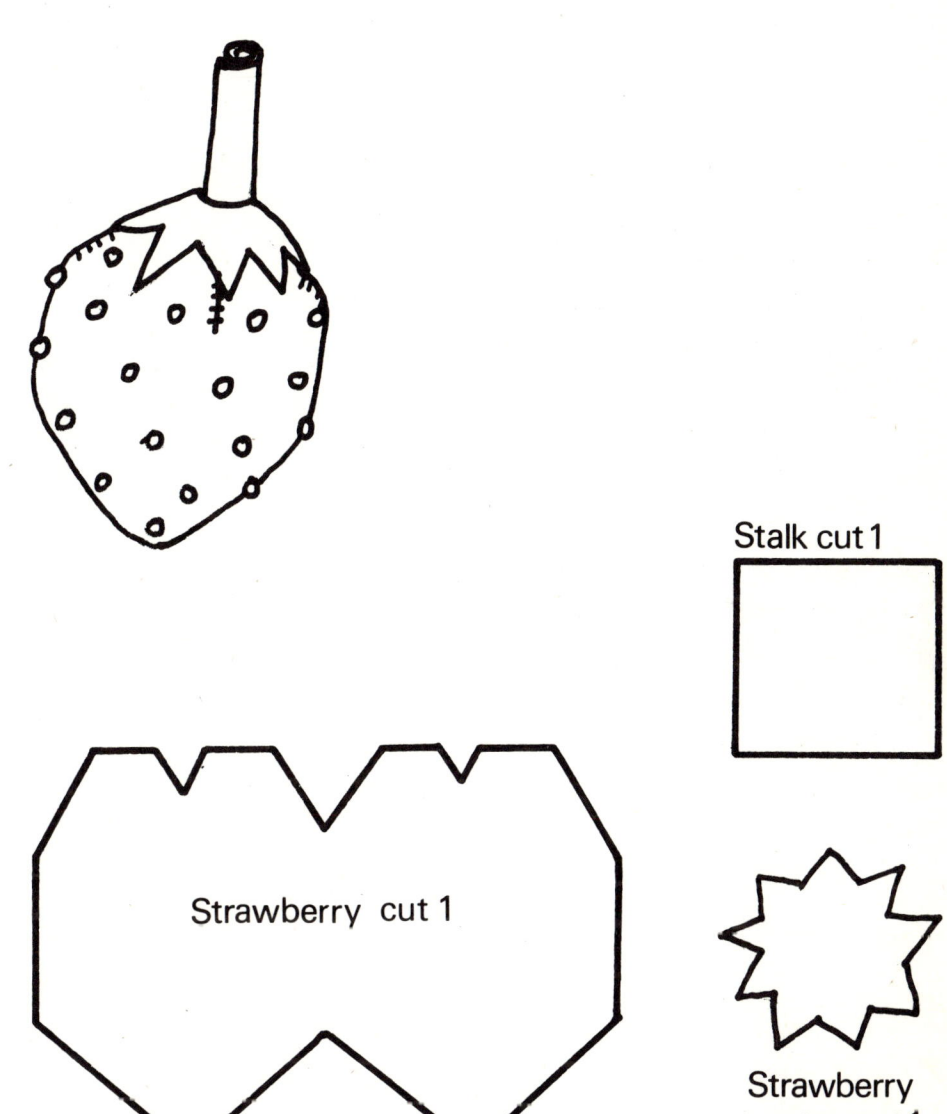

Stalk cut 1

Strawberry cut 1

Strawberry
centre cut 1

Cherries

Cerise or dark red and dark green felt. Stuffing.

Cut two cherries in cerise.

Cut one stalk in green.

Cut two leaves in green.

Roll the stalk up lengthwise and sew along the edge to make the stalk; sew the two leaves at the top as shown in the drawing.

Sew a gathering thread around the circles, leaving a small length of thread to pull the circle into shape. Before closing the top of the circle completely, push in a small amount of stuffing and then tighten the gathering thread, leaving just enough space to push in the stalk. This is then sewn securely in place and the other cherry completed in the same way to make the pair.

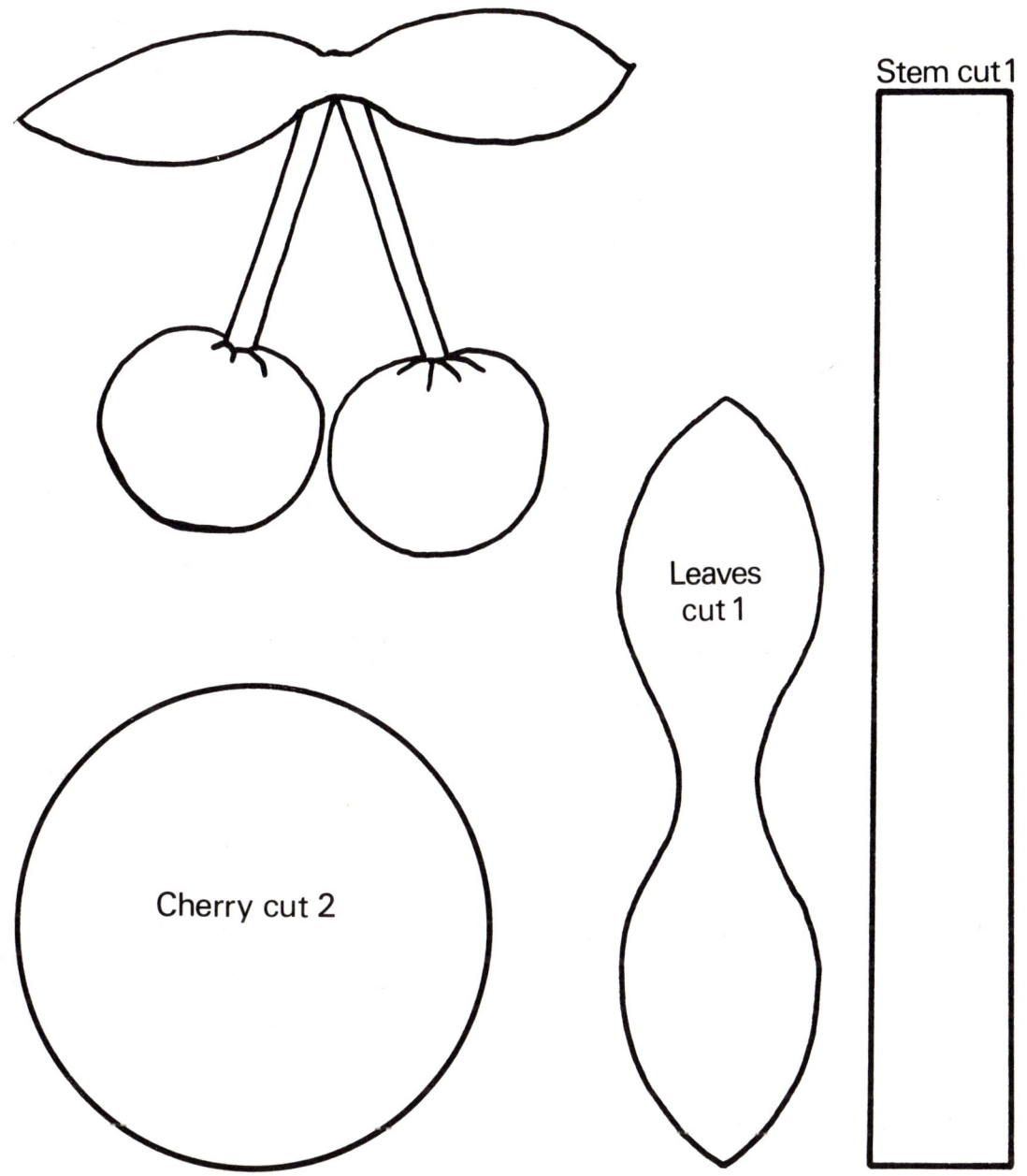

Stem cut 1

Leaves
cut 1

Cherry cut 2

Pear

Pale green and dark green felt. Stuffing. A few dark green shiny beads.

Cut two pear shapes in pale green.

Cut one stalk in dark green.

Cut one pear stalk in dark green.

Cut one pear bottom in dark green.

Sew the darts at the top and the bottom of the pear. Oversew round the two halves leaving a small opening for the stuffing. Stuff so that it is still fairly flat and sew the remaining opening.

Roll the stalk and sew along the edge. Sew it onto the top of the pear and sew the two leaves in front.

Define the leaf veins by stitching a few dark green shiny beads into place along the length.

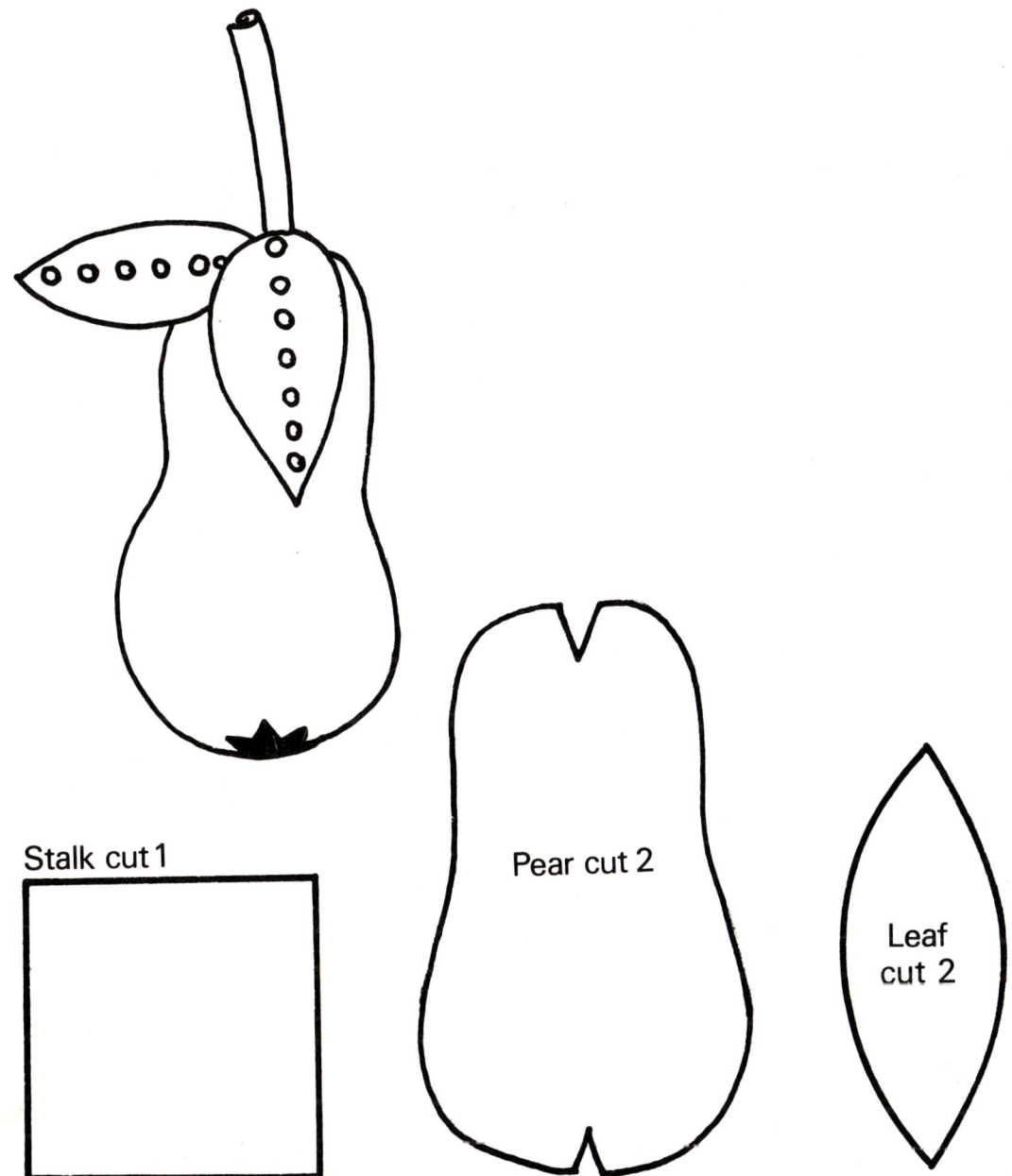

Stalk cut 1

Pear cut 2

Leaf
cut 2

Carrot

Orange and green felt. Stuffing.

Cut two carrots in orange felt.

Cut one carrot top in green.

Sew up the sides of the carrot and push in a little stuffing. Roll the carrot top and cut down to fringe it, then sew it inside the top of the carrot making sure it is quite secure.

All these items can have small gilt safety pins sewn on the back to be worn as brooches or they can be sewn straight onto the garment; do not forget to take them off before washing.

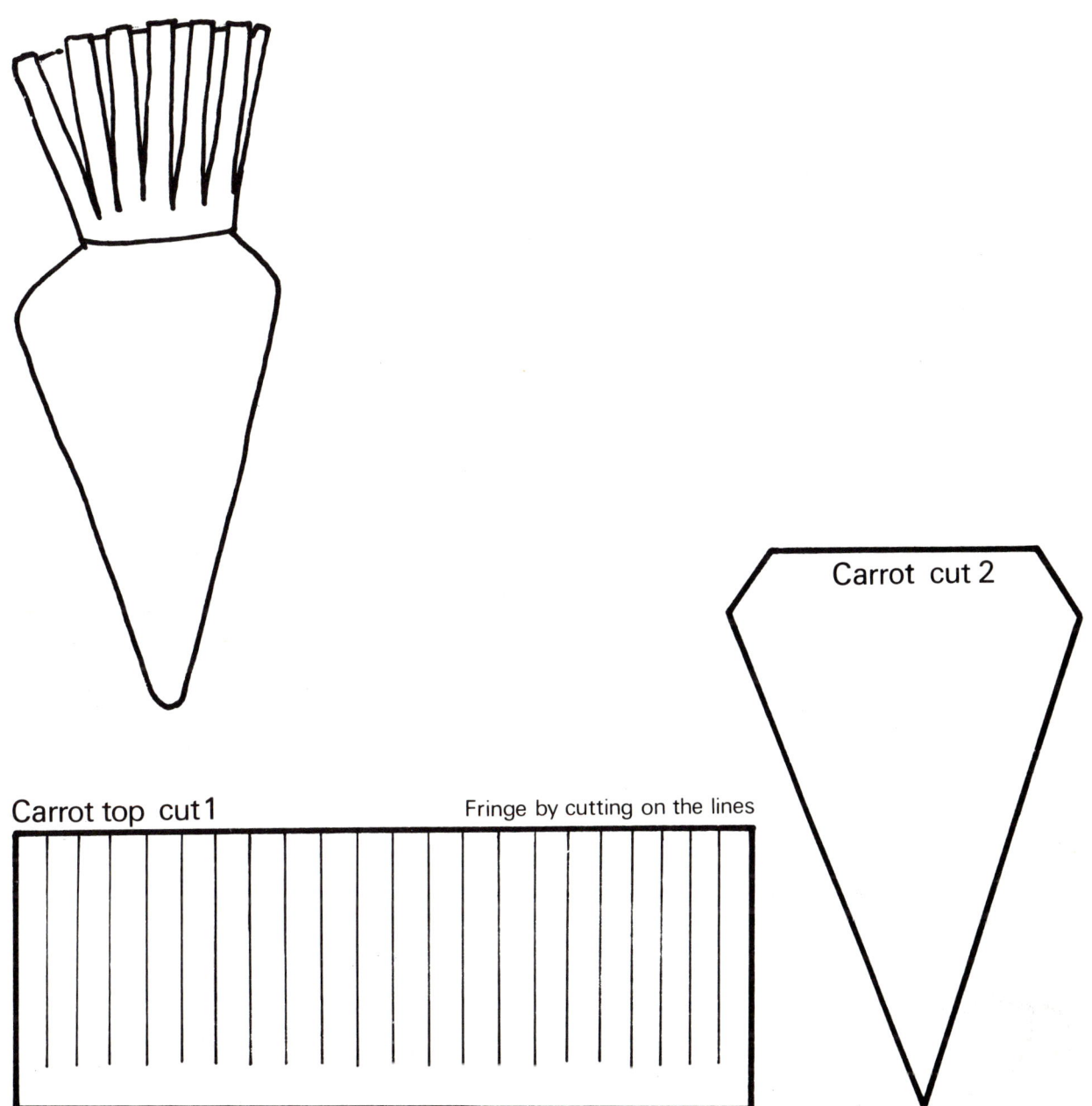

Carrot cut 2

Carrot top cut 1   Fringe by cutting on the lines

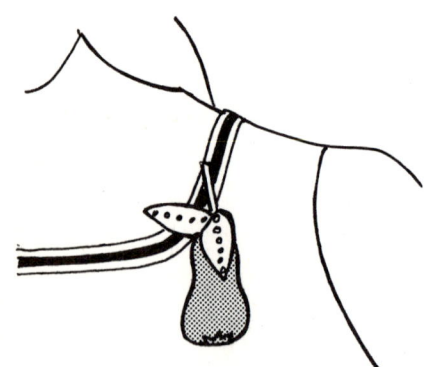

Christmas Tree Decorations

Christmas tree decorations made from felt can look bright and colourful besides having the advantage of not breaking. They are a welcome change from bought decorations and making them can involve even the smallest members of the family.

The simplest decoration needs no sewing at all. Buy a polystyrene ball of the sort used for flower decorations. It can be covered in felt in sections like making a stuffed ball (see illustration on page 44). The six sections are elliptical; simply push pins through the felt into the ball to hold them in place. If the spacing of the pins is even, the pins themselves become part of the decoration. Finally push a pin through a small piece of ribbon into the ball to hang it up. Pins can be pushed through sequins to form patterns or small beads.

Tree decorations using buttons, beads and embroidery

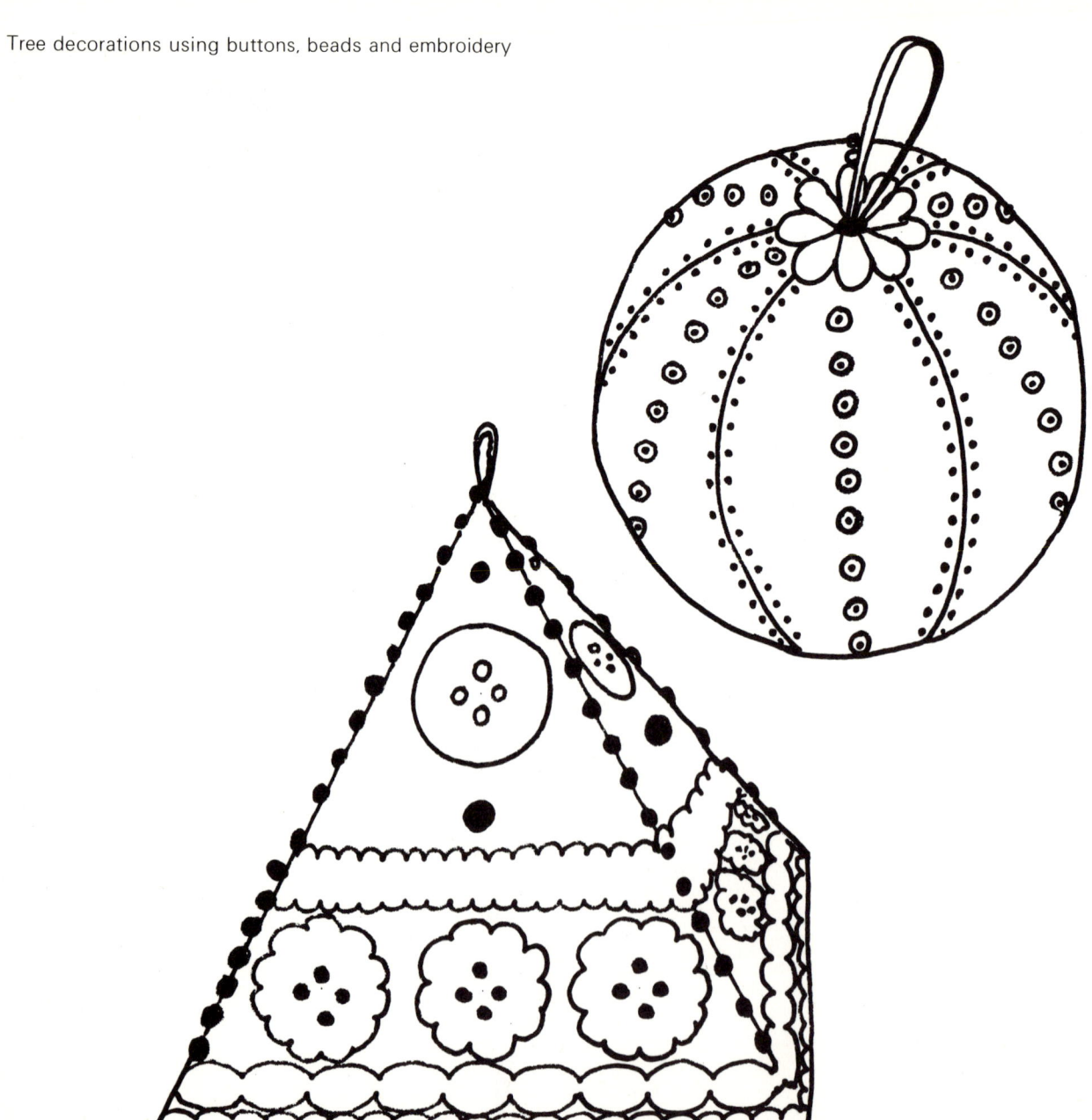

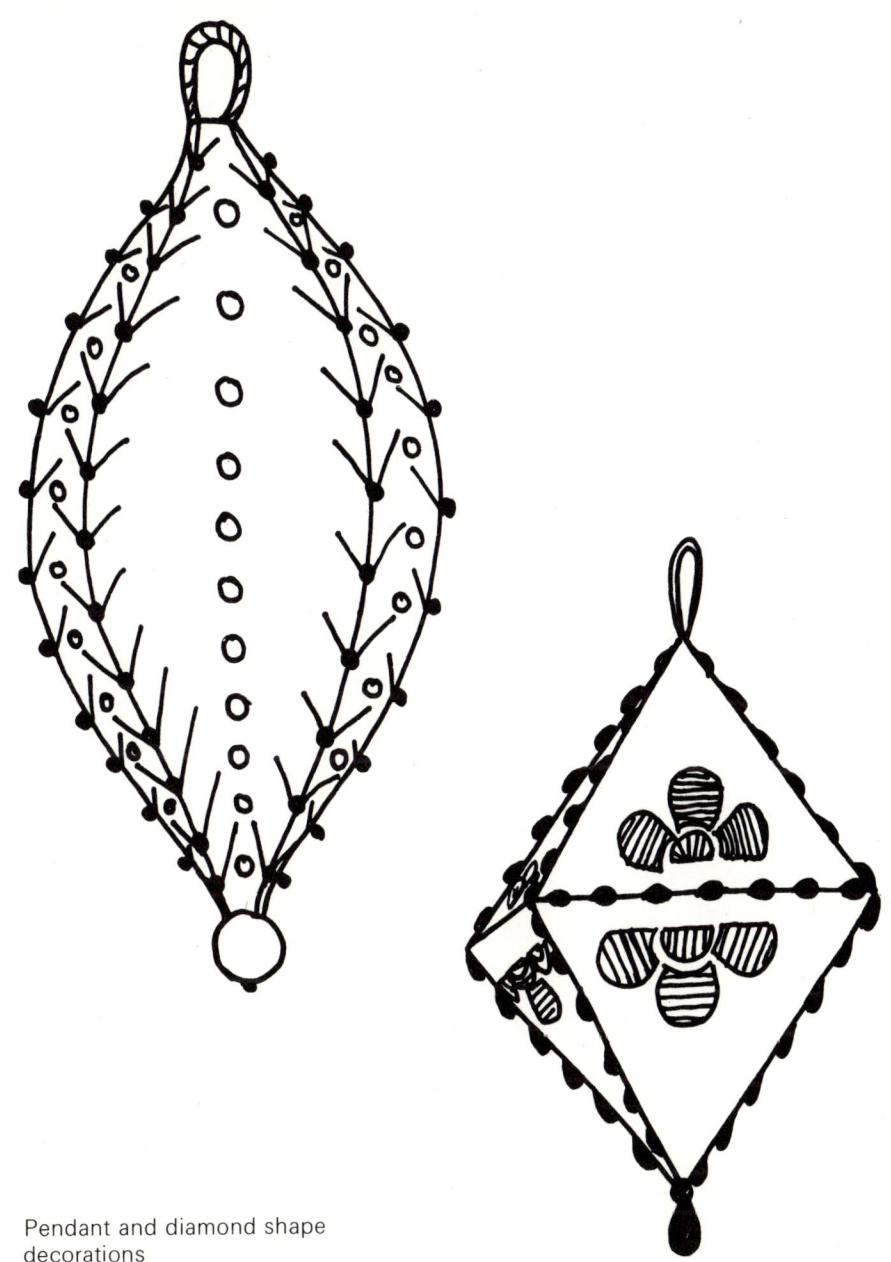

Pendant and diamond shape
decorations

45

The first sewn decoration is a pyramid. Cut the pieces using the trace pattern opposite. One triangular base and three triangular sides are needed. Sew the sides to the base first and then sew up the sides leaving a small opening to push the stuffing in. Make a loop on the top in buttonhole stitch, or sew on a small piece of narrow tape in a matching colour.

Decorations can be added in your own designs, using buttons, beads, sequins, or gold braid. All these can be used to enrich the basic shape.

An extension of the pyramid is to make two units without a base and sew them together as shown on page 45. It can then be decorated in the same way as suggested above.

To make an elongated ball shown in the illustration on page 45, use five pieces of felt cut from the pattern opposite. Sew it section to section, leaving a small opening, then stuff and sew up. Decorate in your own way, perhaps adding a bead to the bottom to make a pendant.

There are many variations that will make each item unique without the need to alter the pattern shapes drastically. Broken bead necklaces, metallic yarns and shiny buttons are useful decorations, besides stones out of cheap jewellery if they are stuck on with a really strong glue, e.g. *UHU* or *Bostik*.

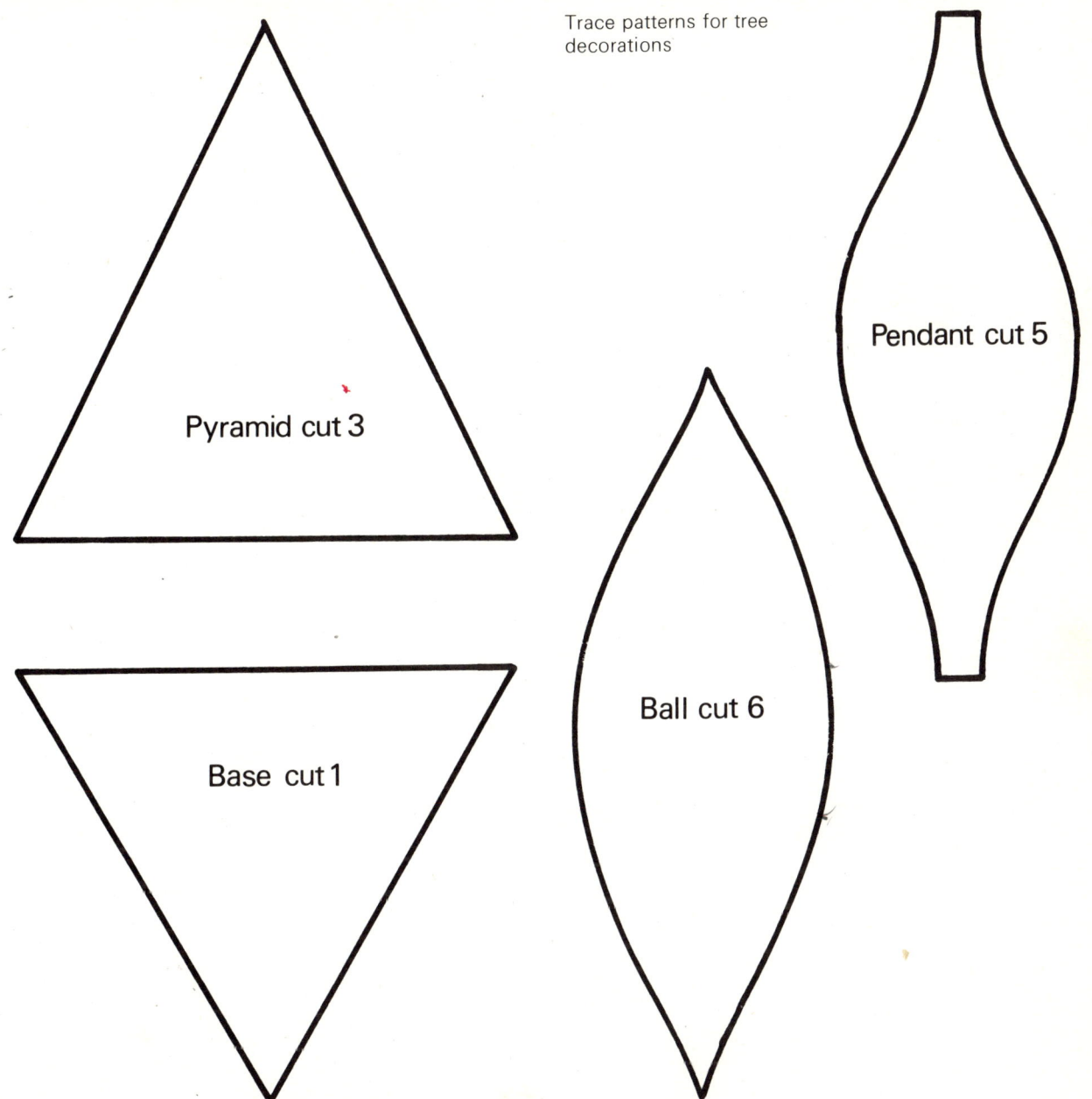

Trace patterns for tree decorations

Pyramid cut 3

Base cut 1

Ball cut 6

Pendant cut 5

47

The Christmas bells opposite are made from two pieces of felt cut to shape and sewn together. The decoration is added afterwards. The basic shapes can be embroidered, have ribbon, beads, gold or silver braid sewn on in stripes or even simple bows of ribbon to make distinctive decorations.

Use the trace pattern opposite to make a paper pattern.

Cut out two bell shapes from any colour felt you choose, place the two shapes together and oversew the edges neatly with matching embroidery thread, leaving a small gap to push in the stuffing. When you stuff the bell don't put too much in, spread it evenly and sew up the gap.

Sew a length of ribbon to the top of the bell to hang it up, then decorate it any way you like.

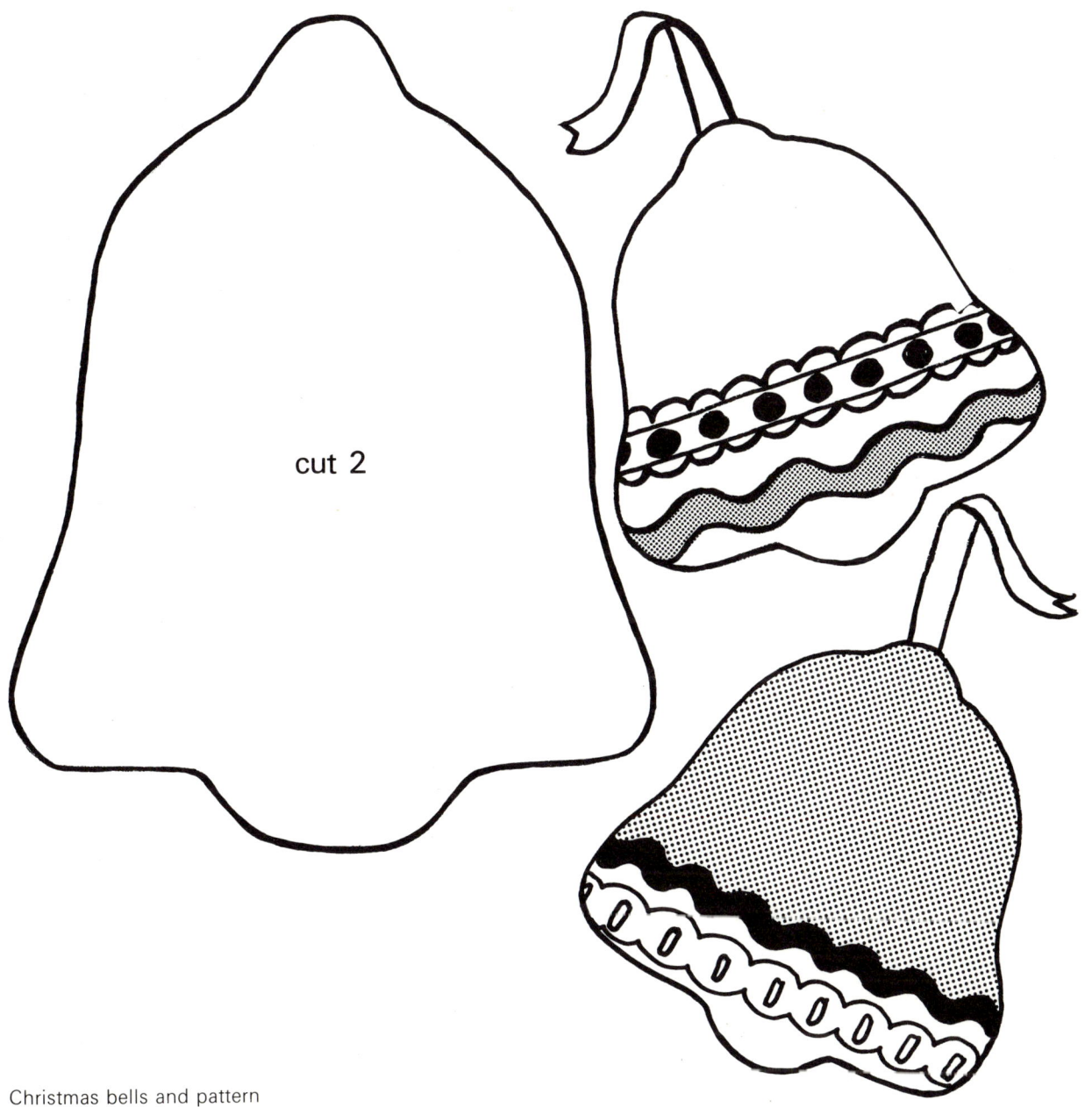

cut 2

Christmas bells and pattern

Felt Toys

Small felt toys can be very satisfying to make, inexpensive and in great demand from small children who enjoy collecting them. The easiest toy is the felt ball.

The example illustrated opposite is made of 12 sections. These sections can be the same colour or all different to use up odd pieces left over.

Start to put the ball together by taking one section and pinning five other sections one to each side. This means that one half of the ball is attached together. Now neatly oversew the edges of the five sides, join each of the side sections and sew them.

Make up the other half of the ball in the same way. You will find that the two completed halves fit together or interlock. Oversew these together, but leave one side open. Push stuffing through the gap left, not too hard. To hang the ball, insert a length of ribbon into the opening before sewing it up. Now the complete ball can be embroidered with different stitches to add interest, or felt shapes can be stuck or sewn on. Felt is such an ideal material on which to do simple embroidery stitches, that it is almost impossible to stop once you have started.

The stitches on page 10 can be used to embroider the ball or any of the toys or items in this book.

Drawing and pattern of ball

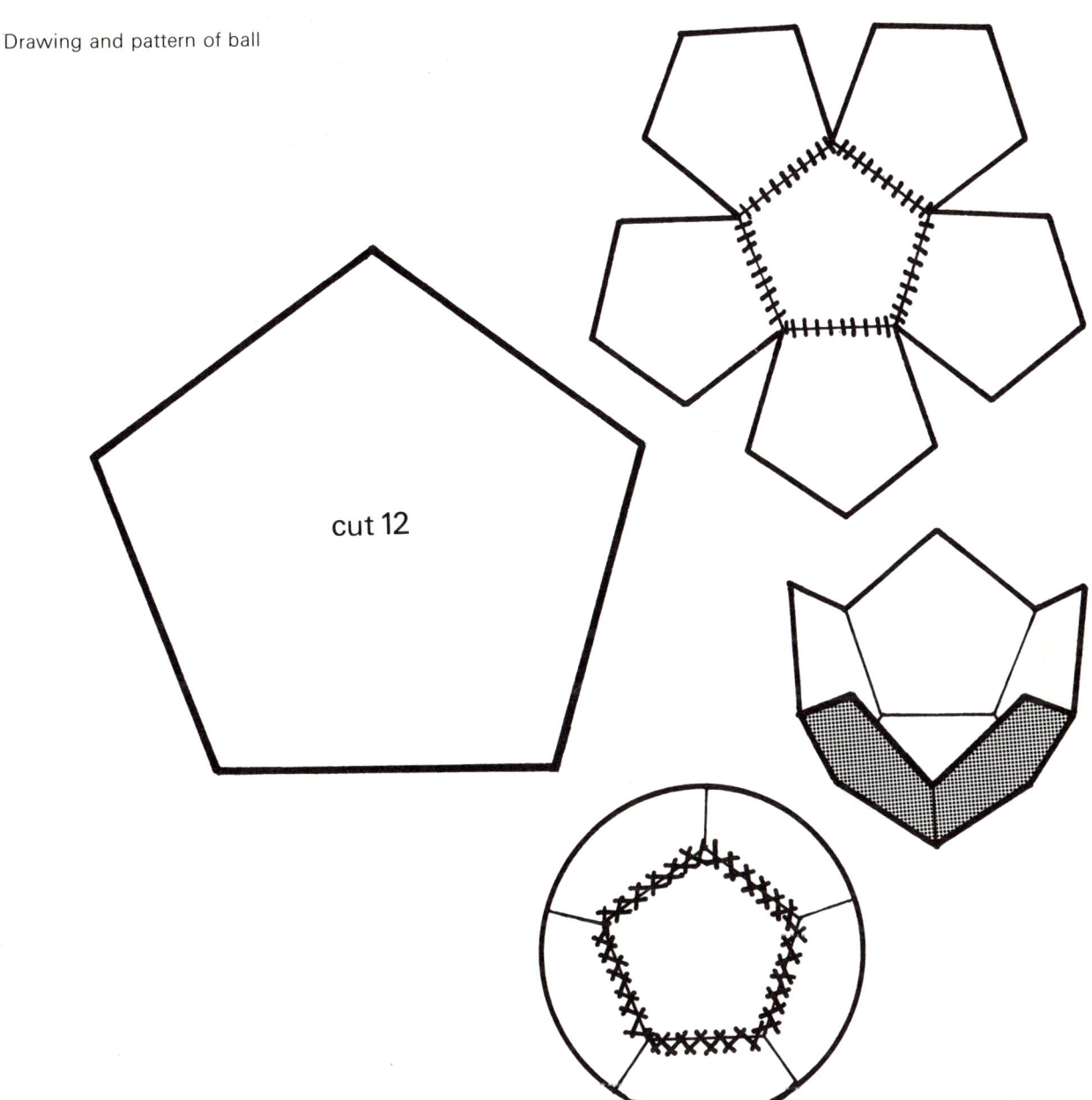

cut 12

Mermaid and Teddy

Teddy is quite small if you make him the size of the pattern shown on page 54 but he could be made bigger. He is made in yellow felt with a blue swimming costume.

Trace the shapes from page 54 onto a sheet of thin paper, and cut out the pieces.

Place the Teddy shape onto the yellow felt, and draw round it twice; also place the swimming costume onto the blue felt and draw round it twice. Place the two halves of the Teddy together and oversew round the edges. Leave a small space for stuffing, then push in some kapok or cottonwool with a fine knitting needle or a thin pencil, making sure the stuffing goes right into the arms and the head.

Sew up the opening and embroider the features with black thread, using satin stitch for the eyes and stem stitch for the nose.

Place the swimming costume one piece on each side and sew up the sides while the Teddy is in it; sew up the shoulder straps.

Cut out some minute scraps of white felt for sails and a piece in black for the little boat motif on his front. Stick it on with glue.

The Teddy could have a pin sewn on his back to make him into a brooch, or he could be sewn on to a bag or hat.

The mermaid opposite is made in different shades of green and blue felt. She can be made larger, but personally I think she is right quite small. I have made several different versions of the mermaid, some with sequins sewn on and metallic yarn for hair. All of them have become mascots and are taken by their owners wherever they go.

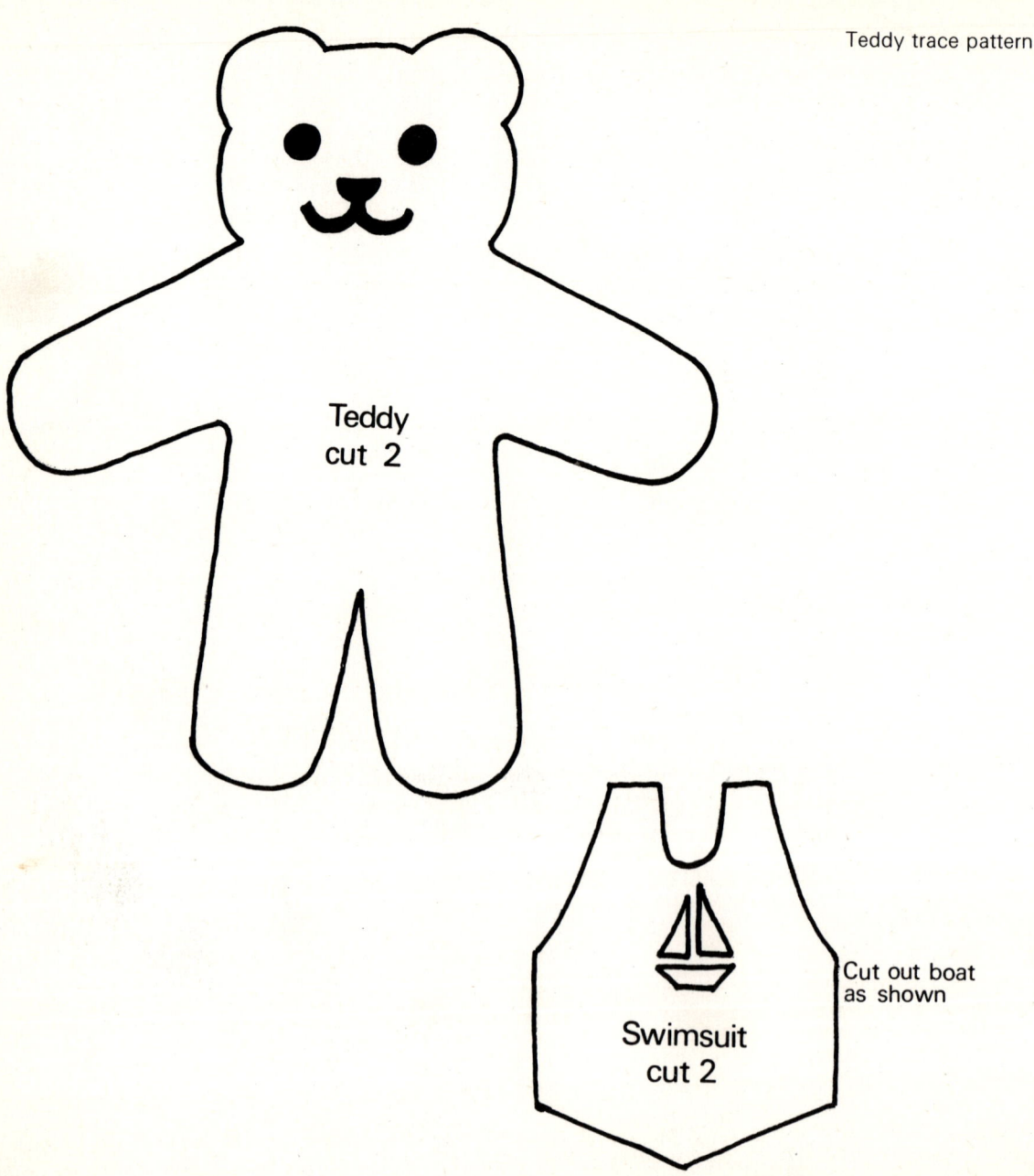

Teddy trace pattern

Teddy
cut 2

Swimsuit
cut 2

Cut out boat
as shown

Mermaid trace pattern

To make the mermaid, trace the pattern pieces onto thin paper and cut them out. The materials needed are: a big piece of felt in blue about 230 mm (9 in.), scraps of bright green and blue felt and also some bright green wool.

Cut out two main sections in blue.

Cut eyes and bust from bright green felt — the scales are different shades of blue and green.

Sew up the two halves, leaving a small opening for stuffing. Stuff firmly, but not too hard. Sew up the gap.

Stick or sew on the bust and eyes and stick or sew on the scales, leaving a gap between each row of scales.

Embroider a mouth with pink yarn or stick on a pink felt mouth.

Finally, cut about eighteen 150 mm (6 in.) lengths of green wool, tie them firmly in the middle and sew to the centre of the mermaid's head.

The peasant lady on page 58 is of vague European origin in appearance. The basic doll shape could be adapted to make a doll of any nationality. Only the most striking characteristics should be used: a lace hat, embroidered waistcoat and relevant colours to suit the country chosen. Make sure that the details are kept in scale.

To make the peasant lady, who is free standing, a 350 mm (13½ in.) square of bright pink felt will be sufficient.

The materials needed are:

small piece of beige felt for the face and hands

small piece of purple felt for the shawl

small piece of white felt for the apron

small scraps in different colours for the head-dress.

Bought braid is used to trim the apron, the hem and waist. 460 mm (18 in.) is enough of the main braid, while the other piece round the apron is only 150 mm (6 in.).

Trace the pattern pieces from pages 59 to 61.

Cut four beige hands and one beige face.

Cut one purple shawl.

Cut one white apron.

Cut two pink body sections.

Cut one pink skirt.

Cut one pink base.

Sew the hands together in pairs and sew round the edges with matching thread.

Put the face in position on one body piece and sew in place. Embroider the eyes with black thread using small satin stitches; make the hair by sewing longer satin stitches. For the mouth use pink thread and small stem stitch.

Place the two body pieces together, and pin in the hands before starting to sew.

With a neat oversewing stitch, go carefully round leaving only the waist seam unsewn. Cotton wool, kapok or fibre filling can be used to stuff the doll.

Peasant lady approx 150 mm
(6 in.) high when finished

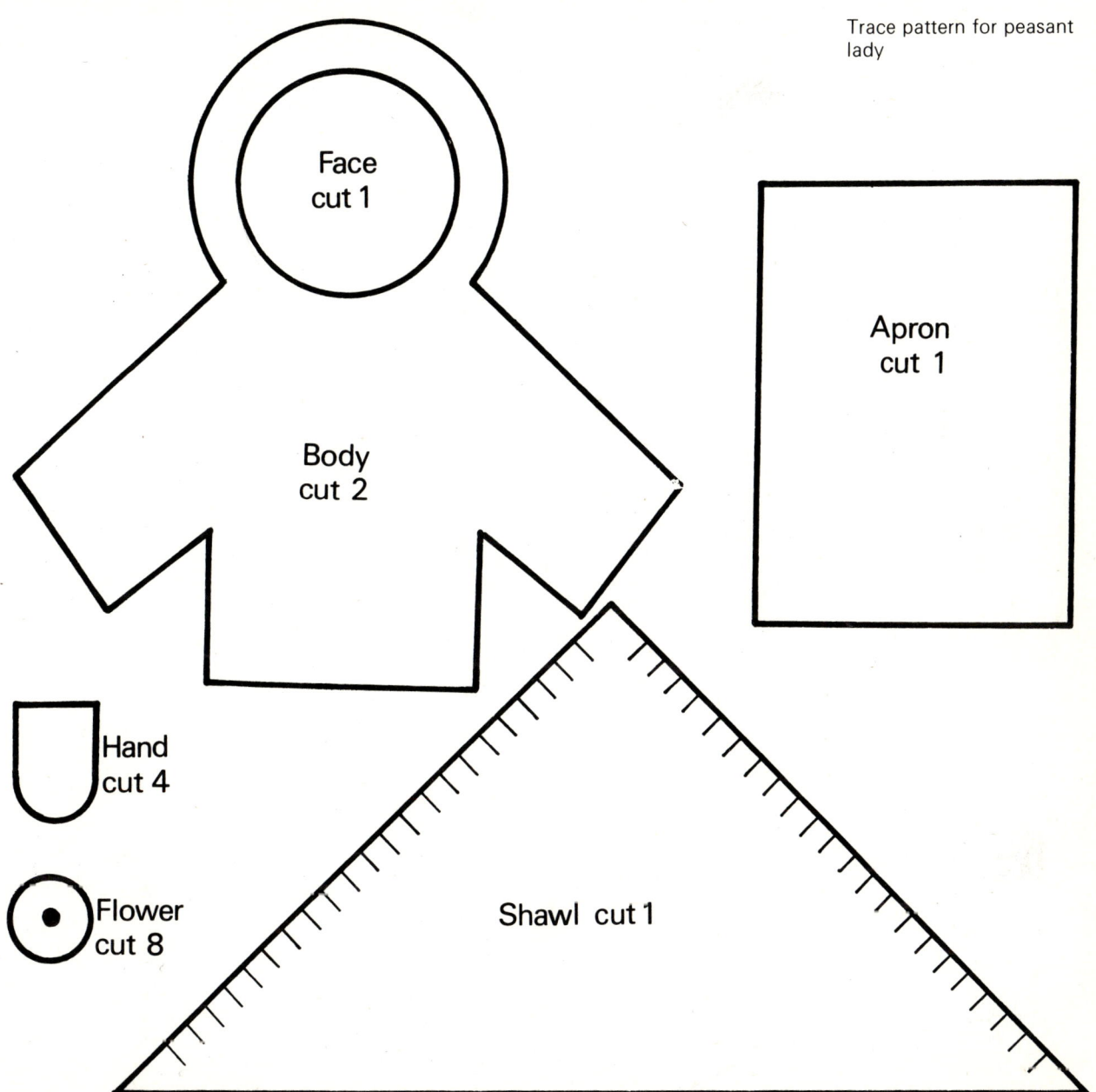

Face
cut 1

Trace pattern for peasant lady

Body
cut 2

Apron
cut 1

Hand
cut 4

Flower
cut 8

Shawl cut 1

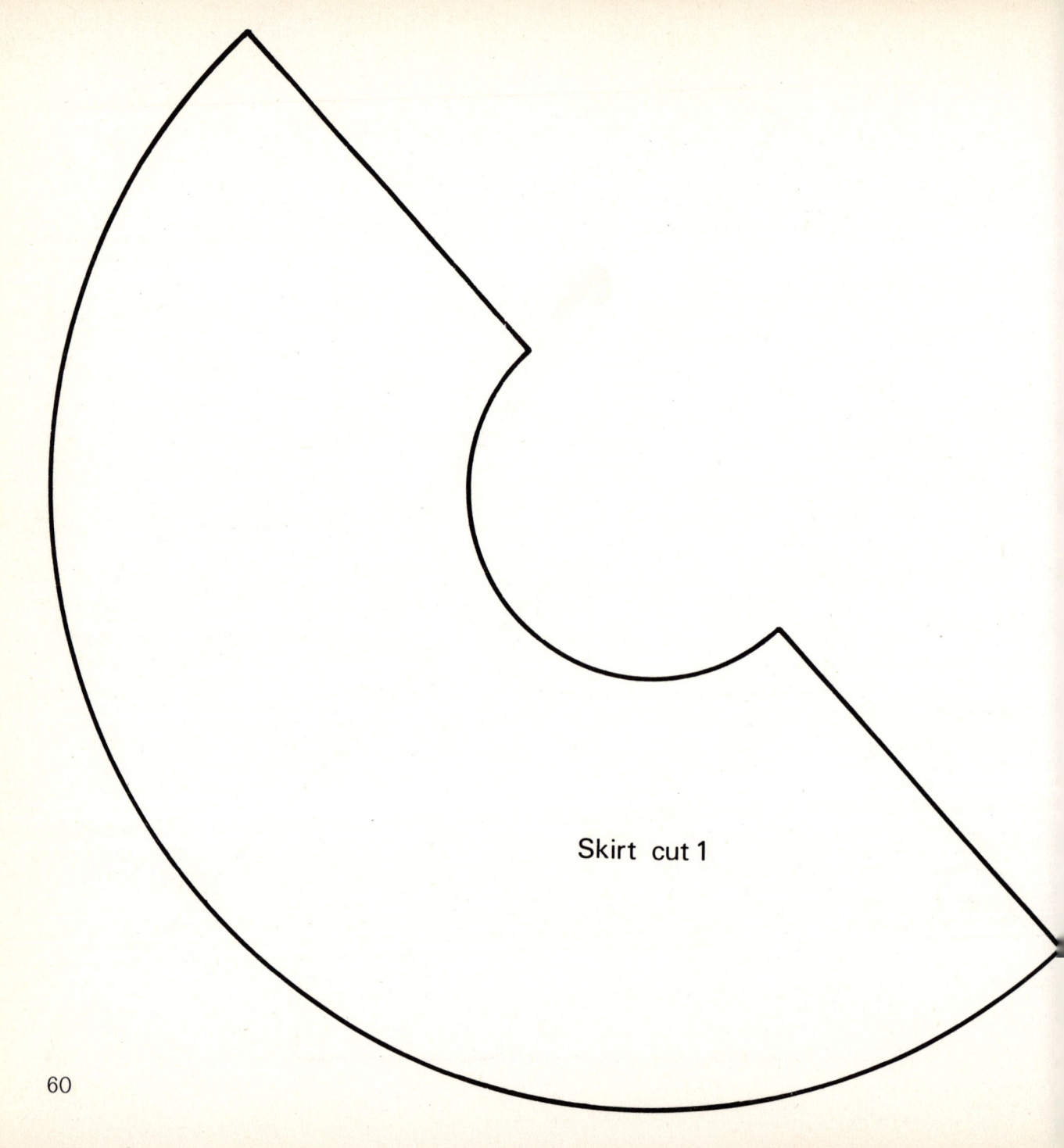

Skirt cut 1

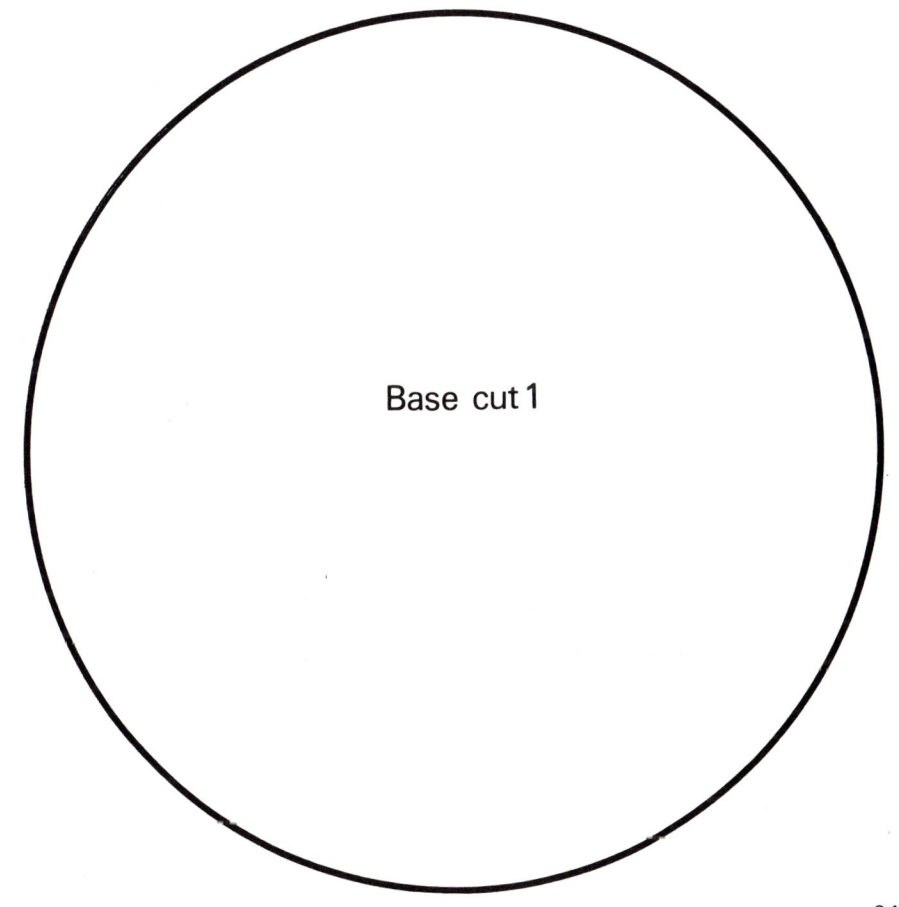

Base cut 1

Begin to stuff the top section, push in some stuffing with a needle or pencil, making sure it goes right into the ends of the arms. Finish the stuffing and catch the waist edge together.

Take the skirt section and sew up the back seam. Pin in the base and oversew it in place.

Push stuffing through the waist of the completed skirt until it is very firm, but not so that it makes the bottom rounded.

Push the body into the skirt and pin in place. Sew firmly in position.

Take the apron and the smaller length of braid, pin it round three edges and sew.

Place the apron on the lady's waist and sew in place.

Take the other length of braid and pin it around the hem of her skirt, sewing it lightly in place. Put a piece of braid around the waist to cover the join of the apron, and sew this.

The purple shawl should have a small fringe cut round two sides as shown in the pattern before it is positioned round the lady's shoulders; catch it lightly in place at the waist.

Finish the doll by making small flowers from circles of different coloured felt. Place the circles round her head and secure each one in place by a French knot at the centre.

The dolls on pages 64 to 66 are made using the basic pattern for the peasant lady. *The Swedish doll* is made in red felt and has long blonde wool plaits and a black hat with an edging of red ribbon. The flowered collar can be made from patterned fabric or have flowers embroidered onto white felt. Add a strip of lace beneath it down to the waist. Make the long apron from red, black and white fabric. The purse is embroidered in red and black and attached to two lengths of ribbon, this is fastened to the waist over the apron with a scarlet waistband.

Make the *Dutch doll* in red too as she is similar to the Swedish one. Make a long plain white apron and fasten it to the waist with patterned ribbon. Add a patterned lace bib at the neck. The white hat is made with a back section sewn in, attach it lightly to the head.

The Spanish doll should be made in emerald green felt. Cut a scarlet scarf and sew it in place with a sparkly bead. Cut two frills in black from the pattern and sew these round the top of the shoulder as in the drawing. The frills round the skirt are the same pattern, just extend it to make 4 frills, sew these on slightly overlapping with the bottom frill extending a little over the base of the doll.

The mantilla is a small piece of black lace attached to the comb which is cut from felt. Make a yellow or pink flower by placing the smaller shape over the top of the larger one using the pattern, sew this on the front of the comb. Sew the comb firmly on the doll's head.

The ideas for costume dolls are very simple, you will certainly want to add many touches of your own. Embroidery beads, lace, feathers, all sorts of ideas will occur as you are dressing them.

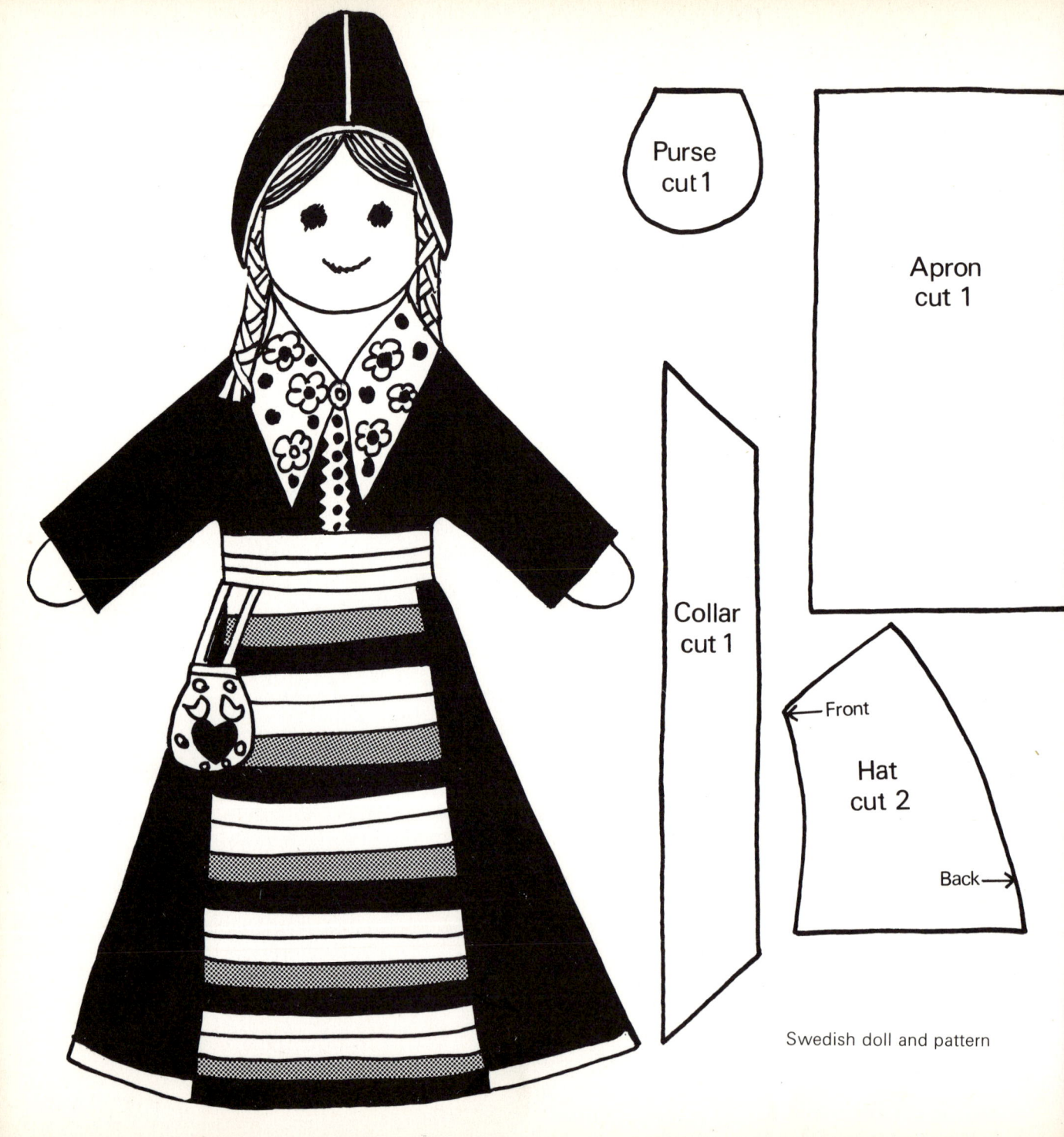

Purse cut 1

Apron cut 1

Collar cut 1

Hat cut 2

Front

Back

Swedish doll and pattern

Scarf cut 1

Comb
cut 1

Flower
cut 1

Frill cut 2

Flower centre
cut 1

Spanish doll and pattern

65

Dutch doll and pattern

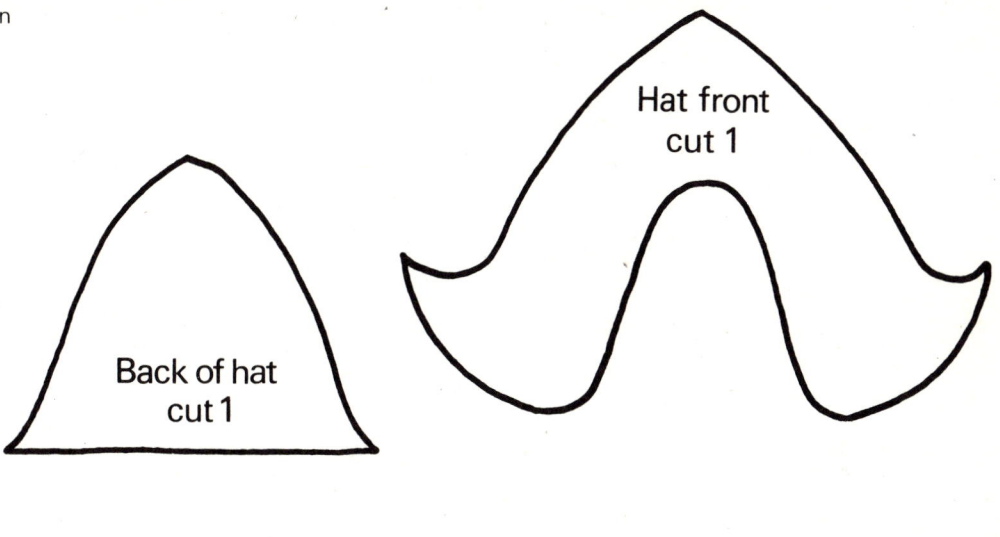

Hat front
cut 1

Back of hat
cut 1

Bib
cut 1

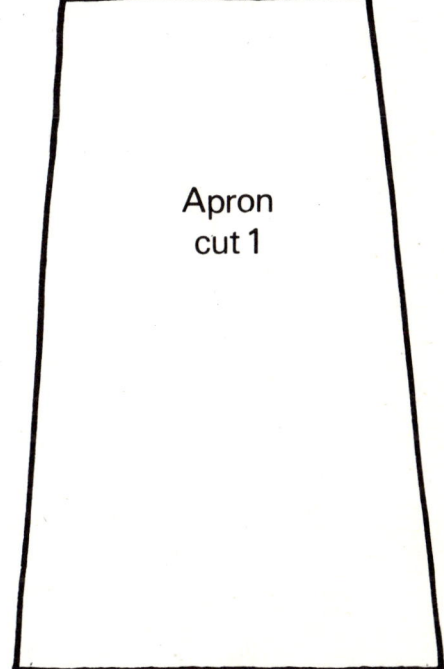

Apron
cut 1

A basic felt doll is an easy toy to make and it can be dressed up in so many ways depending on how much time can be spent on it.

The trace patterns on pages 70 and 71 give the basic shape: cut two out in either flesh pink or beige and oversew the edges neatly. Leave a small opening and push some stuffing firmly into all the limbs. Sew up the opening.

Embroider the eyes and mouth with coloured thread, using simple stem stitch for the mouth and satin stitch for the eyes.

The hair is made by sewing big loops of thick black wool into the head with a needle. Make loops all around the face and the head until every space is covered.

Clothes for this doll are very simple to make. Use the pattern on page 71 to make the dress; cut two shapes out and stitch them together. Add a bit of braid or decorative ribbon for the simplest of dresses. With some imagination the doll can be made in different coloured felt and every one can have a different national costume. Add small touches of beads or trimming, and you can create a whole range of exclusive costume dolls.

Basic felt doll

Body
cut 2

Doll trace pattern

Dress for felt doll

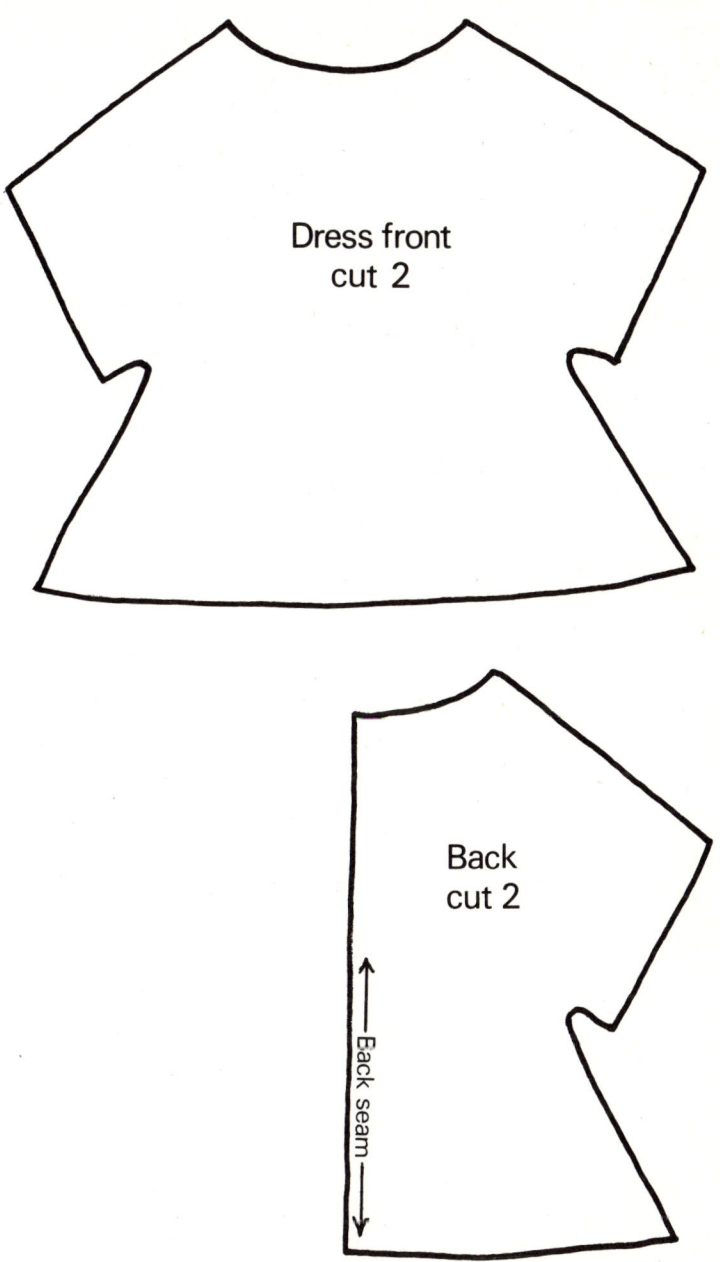

Dress front
cut 2

Back
cut 2

← Back seam →

Greeting Cards

Greetings cards are simply made using felt for the design. They look professional and very bright. One or two simple designs like those illustrated can continue to be used for different people for a long time, with many variations.

Make a card from thin poster card or even the unprinted back of an old card.

Score the centre line neatly and fold it in half.

Plan out the design very lightly on the card with a soft pencil and cut the felt out. Arrange the pieces on it and stick them down with a strong glue.

If shapes are cut out at random from the felt, arrange them on the card first to get the best positions. It is often best to cut the shapes larger than planned originally as there is a tendency to cut things smaller, and then the shapes look lost on a sea of card.

Calendars can be made in the same way, except that the card does not need to be folded. A measuring chart for the wall, so that children can see how much they have grown, could be made in the same way as the cards and calendar. Big motifs and thick lines drawn with a felt-tip pen on a piece of heavy card would make a striking and unusual chart.

Stuck appliqué greeting
cards

Using the drawing of spring flowers to make a special card, trace the shapes accurately before cutting them out in felt

Christmas Cards

Christmas cards are very effective and crisp made in felt appliqué on card. The possibilities in their design are endless as long as the shapes are kept very simple. The first example is a Christmas tree design cut out in bright green and stuck centrally on to a dark blue or black card. To make an extra eye-catching card, add to this a red tub, yellow stars and a few large sequins stuck on for baubles.

There are many variations on the Santa Claus theme that can be tried. An old card with a good simple shape of a Santa can be used to draw round, to make a stuck appliqué as shown on page 76.

Shaped cards need working out on paper first. The example on page 77 is very simple. Draw round the bell on to card and repeat the shape as shown. Score down the centre to fold it in half. Cut one bell shape in red felt and glue it firmly onto the front of the card. Stick on triangle shapes as in the illustration, or stick sequins in gold or silver in a pattern, to complete it.

Christmas cards, stuck felt appliquéd with sequins on the tree, and cotton wool on Santa's beard

Bell shaped Christmas card with stuck felt appliqué

Cushions

Scatter cushions can be made in felt, but remember that they will always have to be dry-cleaned, so choose a suitable filling, not foam. The designs illustrated show simple patterns that can be worked out either on paper or by cutting out and positioning directly onto the felt ground. For a simple design to try first, the sun motif can be used. The basic rectangle for the back and front of the cushion could be cut out in purple felt. Take any strips of felt in shades of pink, violet or pale green. Cut long irregular slivers and lay them slightly overlapping each other about two-thirds of the way up the rectangle. Now machine or hand-stitch them into place.

Cut a large bright red sun and appliqué this centrally over the strips.

If a more decorated finish is desired, embellish the sun with fancy embroidery stitches, but place them inside the shape to emphasise it. (For several embroidery stitches see page 10.)

Shaped cushions need an inner bag to hold the filling material. Make a paper pattern for this bag exactly the same size as the cover. To fasten these felt cushions after inserting the filling, it is best to sew them up neatly with matching thread. Other methods of closing the gap seem to stretch the felt and are easily pulled open.

Two simple designs for
cushions

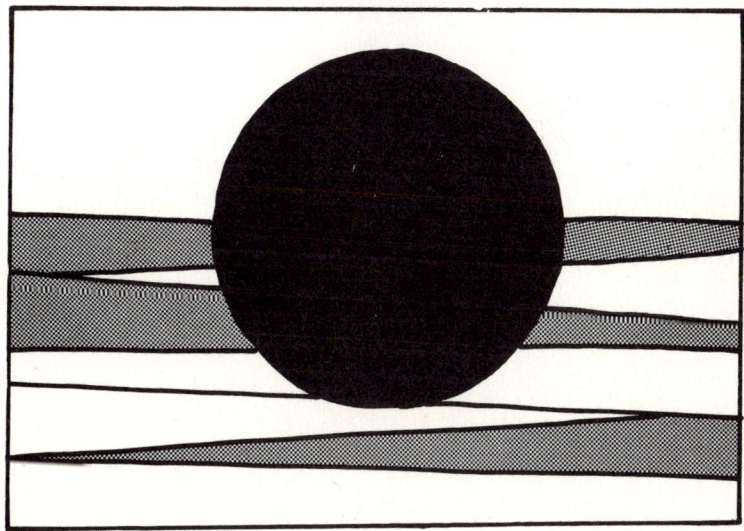

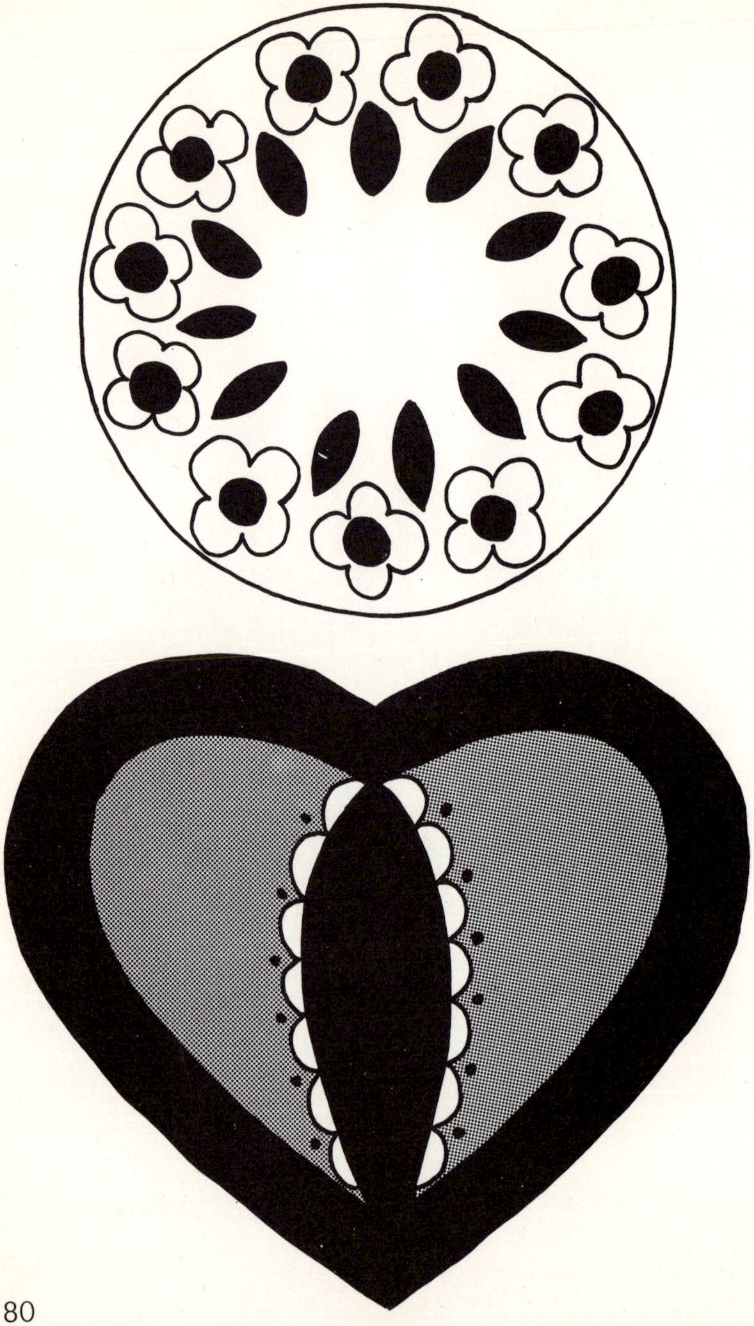

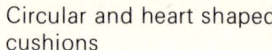

Circular and heart shaped
cushions